LET HERBS DO IT

LET HERBS DO IT

A collection of anecdotes and cooking suggestions to enliven the use of 26 herbs which should be staples in every kitchen

Virginia Williams Bentley

Illustrated by Robin Rothman

Houghton Mifflin Company Boston

1973

Copyright © 1971, 1973 by Virginia Williams Bentley

All rights reserved.

ISBN: 0-395-15478-2
Library of Congress Catalog Card Number: 72-6805
Printed in the United States of America

First Printing M

To Carol who conned,
Gladys who calmed, and
Emma Lou who corrected me.

Contents

Introduction, Page IX

Anise	1	Pepper	65
Basil	5	Poppy	69
Bay	9	Rosemary	73
Caraway	13	Saffron	77
Cardamom	17	Sage	81
Celery	21	Savory	85
Coriander	25	Sesame	89
Dill	29	Tarragon	93
Fennel	33	Thyme	97
Lemon	37	Vanilla	101
Marjoram	41		
Mint	45	Things to Remember About Herbs	105
Mustard	49	Herb Jelly	106
Onion	53	Herb Tea	107
Oregano	57	Index of Recipes	109
Parsley	61		

Introduction

The title of this book is purposely light-hearted, to indicate that herbs are fun: fun to raise, both outdoors and in; fun to cook with; fun to know a little about historically. So each herb is given this three-way treatment.

Someone has said that an impressive array of herbs, on display for all to see, on the kitchen wall, makes even the poorest cook <u>appear</u> to be a gourmet. My aim is to take certain basic herbs out of the display class, get them dusted off and into some tempting dishes.

For reasons difficult to explain, many herbs have gone through a long period of being neglected in this country. You may search in vain in 19th and early 20th century cook books, especially in New England, and find only the blandest of seasonings, except for sage and mustard and a few others. Then, after World War II, came the great change. Herb and spice books have been pouring off the presses ever since; and <u>two hundred million pounds</u> of herbs and spices are now consumed annually in the U.S.A. Fifty years ago it was difficult to find half a dozen seasonings in a grocery store. Now one is confronted by a staggering array. (Long ago, when herbs and spices had enormous popularity, they even gave the "grocer" his name because he bought them by the "gross.") Things seem to have come full circle.

This booklet does not pretend to be definitive in any way. It came about as a result of my agreeing to give a talk to The Forks of the Delaware Garden Club in November 1971. This caused me to search my mind as to what I considered the basics: What did I grow in my own garden, nurture through the winter on a window sill? What herbs of the many on the narrow shelves that adorn my kitchen wall did I actually use the most? (Here herbs and spices are alphabetically arranged for convenience, and, I trust, cause people to think I am a gourmet.)

I came up with a list of 26 things that should be in every kitchen at all times. (This is one woman's opinion. Your list might differ.) Some of them are not technically herbs, but are important seasonings such as lemon and pepper and vanilla, about which I have special phobias. A few spices have crept in, for it is impossible to talk about one kind of seasoning without finding oneself roaming in the camp of the other. It is also difficult to talk of herbs in food without touching on their medicinal qualities, both ancient and modern. Herbs and spices seem to have started as medicines, as preservatives, as fragrances, as sorcerers' helpers, and, only last in their evolution, to have landed in the cook-pot.

We owe most of our culinary traditions to the Romans, who are reputed to have brought some 400 herbs to Britain! They, in turn, had learned about these versatile plants from the Indians, Egyptians, Greeks. After having been forgotten in the Dark Ages, the lore of herbs was rediscovered and preserved by monks in the Middle Ages.

As almost every herb/spice of the 26 discussed has been considered an aphrodisiac at one time or another, I have not consistently mentioned this characteristic. Man has looked upon certain foods hopefully (or fearfully) as stimulants to desire, which suggests a possible reason for herbs going out of style in Puritan dominated England and New England. Many herbs and spices were banned "on the supposition they excited passion". One author[*] claims that

---

[*] Consuming Passions by Phillipa Pullar - Little Brown & Co.

English cooking might not have taken a back seat to French, had it not been for the food taboos that were established under Cromwell. Even potatoes were eyed with suspicion: "Eating of these roots doth excite Venus and increaseth lust."

Another reason for the decline in use of herbs (up to recent years) could have been their close partnership with witchcraft. When witchcraft was recognized as ludicrous, perhaps the herbs, through association, lost their popularity also. In the 19th century the Industrial Revolution started mass production of synthetic substitutes for herbs and flavorings, and, in the 20th century, modern refrigeration has helped us to forget the many wonderful powers of natural herbs. Properly cooled, meat no longer needed massive seasoning to mask an over-ripe flavor. Then, too, as modern man took to moving about more, he couldn't be bothered with the lovely discipline of a precise herb garden. The practice of medicine today has pushed herbs aside from their earlier prestigious stance. It seems to be the nature of man to "throw out the baby with the bath water" when new, more convenient methods are developed. It takes only a generation or two for traditional knowledge to be forgotten or lost.

In the early 20th century a few hobbyists were responsible for keeping herb culture alive, and it was usually older people who attended lectures on herbs. Now the very young, with their long hair and granny glasses, swarm to any store or lecture hall or garden that has anything to do with herbs.

The subject of the rediscovery of herbs is an exciting one. Their history is also the history of mankind and older than the use of fire.

In the 26 little summaries about each herb, I have tried to give a few details for the cook's mind to dwell on while using some of mankind's oldest friends.

"Herb" may be pronounced with the "H" or without it. Either way is correct. What is the difference between an herb and a spice? To generalize dangerously: herbs are leafy, aromatic plants, usually grown from seed in the Temperate Zone; spices are more often aromatic barks of trees, or seeds, or buds, grown in the Tropical Zone. There are so many exceptions to every definition that one becomes lost in a confusion of leaves, seeds, barks, roots and vines. Some seasonings start as herbs, and, after going to seed, find themselves listed as spices. The main thing is to enjoy their use. I have concentrated mostly on herbs because people seem less sure of how to use them, and they are as available as one's kitchen garden.

Hippocrates said, "Let foods be your medicine and medicine your foods." Perhaps this little booklet will help you to follow this ancient advice.

The recipes, that go with each of the 26 herbs, are favorites of mine which seem to qualify for my three-way "hang-up": _good_ , _good for you_ , _easy to prepare_.

Virginia Williams Bentley
Danville, Vermont 05828

LET HERBS DO IT

ANISE – called "Tut-Te-See-Hau" by American Indians, meaning "It expels the wind." Native to Mediterranean area. An annual of parsley family. One of oldest plants known. Biblical. One of the four great hot seeds. Roots, leaves, seeds are edible. Has licorice flavor and is often used in place of real licorice. Used by Egyptians and Greeks. Favorite of old Romans, growing wild everywhere. Cultivated by Charlemagne. Spread throughout Europe by Roman legions. 1305: anise listed by King Edward I as liable to toll. Sufficiently popular that this fee was used to help repair London Bridge. Personal linen of Edward IV perfumed with anise. (Not to be confused with "Star Anise" which has similar flavor and comes from small evergreen tree of magnolia family; much used in Chinese cooking.) Easily raised in gardens of Temperate Zone. Not worth bringing in house. Buy the seeds. A medicine, a food, a seasoning. Settles stomach, aids digestion, sweetens breath, loosens coughs, helps asthma; a sedative, diuretic. Basis of anisette, absinthe, Campari. Used in drag hunts, as bait for rats and mice — even as fish lure. Its flowers flavor muscatel wine and vermouth. Used in soaps, perfumes and cough drops. Let this versatile herb be ever at your right hand. "It unbindeth the stopping of the liver and of wicked winds and of great humours."

Anise in Cooking

It has authority. Use sparingly.
Sprinkle a few anise seeds over fruit, cabbage slaw, in fish chowder, in shellfish cooking, on cakes and cookies. Add a touch to baked apples, apple sauce, apple pie — as a refreshing change from cinnamon.

Use ½ teaspoon crushed seed in an 8 ounce package of cream cheese for a canapé spread.

Leaves of fresh anise, frugally used, enhance a green salad.

Make a soothing tea of the seeds for a soporific nightcap. (See back of booklet.)

Use strong, cold Anise Tea to pour over a fruit cup. Sweeten the fruit with honey or maple syrup. Chill well. Serve as dessert! Different, refreshing, healthful.

Fig Conserve
(To serve with meat)

1 pound dried figs
1 teaspoon anise seed, crushed
2 cups water
} soaked together for at least 4 hours and then brought to a boil.

1 cup sugar, added to above when it is boiling, and simmered, uncovered, until syrup is thick, figs tender. Cool.

juice of ½ lemon
¾ cup chopped toasted almonds
} added to cooled fruit above.

A dash of rum may be added, but is optional.

Anise Wafers (makes about 3 dozen)

½ cup soft butter (¼ pound stick) ⎫ well blended together
1 cup sugar   ⎭

1 egg, beaten and added to above
½ teaspoon vanilla added to above mixture

1¾ cups flour   ⎫
½ teaspoon salt   ⎬ mixed well together
1½ teaspoons baking powder ⎬ and thoroughly
1½ teaspoons anise seed, crushed ⎭ stirred into above.

Roll this dough into one-inch balls.
Place on lightly buttered cookie sheet or sheets.
Press down each ball with a buttered fork.
Bake in a preheated 350° oven for about ½ hour or until a pale golden brown. Watch carefully.

The perfect accompaniment to a fresh fruit dessert.

———————

<u>BASIL</u> — sometimes called "<u>Kiss-Me-Nicholas</u>" in various parts of Italy where it is considered a token of love. A girl wearing a sprig of basil suggests her beau need not keep his distance. In Romania if a boy accepts basil from a girl it means he's engaged. An annual plant of the mint family and native to India, Africa, Asia. One of the oldest herbs known to man; considered sacred in India. It's a bursting-with-life herb, basic to every herb garden. Its uses are legion, its loveliness legendary. Pick a fragrant bouquet of it for your house; it sprouts roots while one's back is turned. Reputed to keep flies away and decorative pots of basil adorn the café tables of France and Italy for that reason. Not mentioned in Bible but tradition has it that Salome hid the head of John the Baptist in a pot of basil to give it loving care. She must have had belated regrets. Hindus place basil in the hands of the deceased as a passport to paradise. Jews have, at times, held it in their hands to give strength during religious feasts. Much used in White Magic during Middle Ages.

  Basil is both food and medicine. Considered a powerful tonic, stimulant, nerve remedy. Relieves nausea. Used externally to relieve bites of snakes and spiders. An insecticide.

  Make basil jelly and tea. (See back of booklet.) The tea is especially good for one who is nauseated. By all means grow this delicately lusty herb in both your outdoor and indoor garden. Love and honor it as the Italians do. It is the TOMATO herb par excellence and may be used more generously than oregano.

Basil in Cooking

It is basil with tomatoes in Italy; basil with fish in England.

A <u>must</u> in the green salad bowl, especially with tomatoes, but use it any way.

Basil enhances eggplant, green beans, zucchini, peas, cucumbers.

Gives a great lift to baked macaroni and cheese.

Use the fresh, chopped green leaves if you're a gardener. Use the dried store variety if you're not.

Whether tomatoes are baked, broiled, fresh or in soup — add that touch of basil!

Try basil leaves in a tomato sandwich in place of lettuce.

Parmesan cheese and basil are soul mates. Try broiling tomatoes topped with sweet butter, basil, and a sprinkling of Parmesan cheese.

Mix chopped basil with cream cheese, as a filling for celery, and serve with tomato juice or a "Bloody Mary."

Basil Crab Bisque (Serves 4)

1 can best crabmeat (about ½ pound) Remove all tendons carefully, and flake.
½ cup Sherry, poured over crabmeat and allowed to soak for at least one hour.

1 can condensed green pea soup
1 can condensed tomato soup
¼ teaspoon basil (double if fresh)
¼ teaspoon savory   "   "   "
1 cup milk
1 teaspoon Worcestershire Sauce
} Mix and heat in double boiler.

When mixture in double boiler is well heated, add the crab and Sherry. Allow to heat a few more minutes and serve at once.

(If you prefer a thinner bisque — add a little water.)

Ever so quick and easy and good.

Potato Salad with Cucumbers and Basil
(Serves 6)

½ teaspoon salt
a little freshly ground pepper
6 tablespoons salad oil
} mixed in a fair-sized bowl

2 tablespoons vinegar, added to above, little by little, stirring with a fork all the while.

3 cups sliced, boiled potatoes
½ cup finely sliced, peeled cucumber
} added to above dressing, refrigerated for 2 hours, then drained.

¾ cup mayonnaise
3 tablespoons cream
3 tablespoons finely chopped onion
1 tablespoon chopped fresh basil
(or ½ teaspoon dried basil)
1 teaspoon lemon juice
} mixed and added to above drained potato and cucumber. Correct salt and pepper.

Chill until ready to serve.
Garnish with fresh basil leaves. Lovely!

A Craig Claiborne recipe.

BAY LEAF (Laurel or Laurus nobilis)

Among the most important herbs in today's spice trade. Shades of the Delphic oracle! According to legend, she is alleged to have chewed laurel leaves, or sniffed the smoke from burning laurel, to promote the trances and visions for which she was famous. The laurel is sometimes called the Daphne tree in Greece, since the nymph Daphne, trying to escape the advances of Apollo, was turned into a tree. Native to Mediterranean region and Asia Minor. Buy a potted plant; expensive, but worth it. During the warm summer, keep it in the garden; cherish it by your fireside in winter. Has lovely shiny leaves — the same kind used in garlands made for winners in the Olympic games, from 776 B.C. on. Our word "baccalaureate" means "laurel berries", and signifies successful completion of one's studies, for it alludes to the wreaths worn by poets and scholars receiving academic honors, as well as to triumphant athletes of ancient Greece. Doctors, called "bachelors" in the academic sense, were also crowned with laurel, which was considered a cure-all. Oil of bay (laurel) used for sprains. Leaves once used for tea. Leaves, berries, oil — all have narcotic properties. No relation to bayberry bushes of the American seashore, which are poisonous. Not to be confused with the wild and ornamental laurel of the U.S., which is not edible. Used in Bible Times; Psalm 37:35 says, "I have seen the wicked in great power and spreading himself like a green bay tree." In Middle Ages was believed to induce abortions and to be endowed with many magical qualities. Much used today, ornamentally, in approaches to Italian villas. Lends itself readily to topiary treatment. Why not have your own bay tree, snip it into fancy shapes, and use the clippings for cooking?

Bay Leaf in Cooking

"To win a wreath for your brow
Put a laurel leaf in the stew pot now."

There is more truth to this old verse than poetry, for bay leaf is the basis of "bouquet garni", without which most soups and stews would be a flop. Likewise court bouillon.

Use sparingly. Has an all-pervading strength. Many a dish ruined by too heavy a hand. Often only a small piece of a leaf need be used. A whole bay leaf would only be used in a commodious kettle of soup, as in The Senate Bean Soup which follows.

Bay leaf gives provocative aroma to meats, fish, fowl and pickles. Try a touch in fish chowder, tomato juice, marinades.

Senate Bean Soup (Serves 8)

<u>1 cup dried beans</u> (soldier, pea, yellow eyes, or limas) soaked over night in cold water to cover.

<u>2 quarts</u> (about) <u>of broth</u> from a boiled ham dinner or broth made of leftover roast ham. This must refrigerate over night so all fat can be removed.

<u>1 bay leaf</u>
<u>6 peppercorns</u>
<u>6 whole cloves</u>
} added to beans (after they have soaked and water has been poured off) and the fat-free ham water. Combine all in stewing kettle and let simmer about 2½ hours.

<u>2 carrots</u>, washed and cut up, but not scraped
<u>6 ribs of celery</u>, with a few of the leaves, cut up
<u>1 large onion</u> (or 2 small) cut up
<u>1 large potato</u> (or 2 small) cut up
} added to above and simmered ½ hour more

Allow to cool a bit. Remove bay leaf, peppercorns and cloves. Put soup in blender and blend. (This must be done in installments or blender will overflow.) Test for salt. Thin soup with water if too thick. Add some carefully cut up pieces of <u>leftover ham</u>. Serve with <u>croutons</u>. This soup may be made way ahead of meal and heated at the last minute. It is hearty fare and a reasonable facsimile of the soup served in U.S. Senate dining room; probably better.

Halibut Hollenden (Serves 6)

¼ pound slice of fat salt pork, cut into thin slices and then into small pieces. Arrange these on the bottom of a stove-to-table roasting pan.

1 onion, thinly sliced and spread over salt pork
2 bay leaves, crumbled and sprinkled over above
a 2 pound slice of halibut, placed on the bed of pork-onion-bay

3 tablespoons soft butter
3 tablespoons flour
} creamed together and spread all over the fish, carefully, so as to mask it.

¾ cup buttered saltine crumbs, sprinkled over all.

Cover the dish with a piece of foil. Bake in a preheated 325° oven for one hour. Remove foil and continue to bake until crumbs are brown — about 15 minutes. Garnish with lemon wedges, parsley, paprika. Serve with egg sauce.

Even people who don't like fish like this dish. The bay leaves are the secret.

CARAWAY

— "a tonic for pale girls", according to a First Century Greek physician. Also it is said to destroy "wicked winds and the cough ….. good for the frenzy and the biting of venomous beasts….It restoreth hair where it has fallen away." If you want company to return — serve caraway, according to ancient superstition. A hardy biennial herb of the parsley family. Seeds were found among 5000-year-old debris of Swiss Lake Dwellers. Recorded in 1552 B.C. medical papyrus of Thebes. Believed to have been cultivated longer in Europe than any other condiment. One of the few herbs not indigenous to Middle East. Sometimes called "Roman Cumin"; and because it has more or less replaced cumin today, I have not included cumin in my list of most necessary herbs. The English and Germans seem to have loved it best and used it for over 1000 years. Evidently, in the U.S., it is a runaway from early colonial gardens, growing wild and copiously and resembling Queen Anne's Lace. Not suited as a house plant, but ever so easy to grow outdoors in summer; and the greens give a fillip to the salad bowl. The seeds, the part of the herb most often used, are better purchased, unless you are a purist and like the winnowing process. Caraway seeds are imported chiefly from Netherlands today. Chew the seeds after meals for indigestion. They strengthen and give tone to whole digestive tract. They have anti-bacterial properties. Used in mouthwash, perfume, soap, Kümmel. Caraway "strengthens vision, confers gift of memory." Lovers were once given the seeds to cure fickleness; pigeons were fed the seeds to prevent their straying. The candy covered seeds are known as "comfits." Caraway seeds are sometimes called "whiskey killers," for they mask an alcoholic breath. Considered one of man's best friends. Cultivate this friendship.

Caraway in Cooking

Use the seeds sparingly. They are strong.
Use the tender leaves in salad bowl.
Roots may be boiled for vegetable.
Germans love caraway seeds with cabbage.
So will you.
Make tea from the crushed seeds. (See back of booklet.) Caraway seeds put into bread not only taste good but make the bread more digestible. That was the original purpose of the seeds' use. (Use 1 tablespoon of seeds to a normal bread recipe.)

Try 1 teaspoon of caraway seeds mixed into the pastry for an apple pie!

Good with any apple dish.

Potatoes are enhanced by a dash of caraway.

Add a few seeds to Roquefort salad dressing.

Add to spiced beets, cakes, cookies — and to beef, lamb, or veal stews. Pork and a touch of caraway go well together.

Old time Vermonters remember gathering the wild seeds so their mothers could make caraway seed cookies. A few sensible people still do it. Simply add caraway to any good cookie recipe.

Caraway Spread

1 pound Cheddar cheese, grated, or cut into small pieces
½ cup of beer or ale
2 Tablespoons butter
½ teaspoon garlic salt
1 tablespoon caraway seeds

Heat the cheese, beer, and butter in a saucepan, just until cheese melts, no more. Remove from heat. Add salt and caraway. Beat with an egg beater until thoroughly blended. Pour into ramekins. Refrigerate until ready to use. Serve with rye bread or wheat thins for a truly delicious and different cocktail snack.

Caraway Beets (Serves 4)

1 one-pound can sliced beets, drained (or 2 cups home-cooked)
2 tablespoons butter
1 tablespoon lemon juice
½ teaspoon salt
pepper, freshly ground, a dash
¾ teaspoon caraway seeds
¼ cup sour cream or yogurt

Place all ingredients in a stove-to-table dish of appropriate size. Stir and heat thoroughly but do not boil. Serve at once.

CARDAMOM

(Spelled with M or N for last letter.) Often called "Grains of Paradise." A three-sided wonder and most popular in Middle East where, it is said, a poor man would rather give up his bread than his daily cardamom intake, for three reasons: ① Cools the body in hot weather; ② Aids digestion, relieves indigestion; ③ Is believed to be the best of aphrodisiacs. Other three-way facts about this three-sided seed: ① In the Middle East its chief use is in the daily coffee; ② In Scandinavia its chief use is in baked goods; ③ In the U.S.A. it has been used most extensively by the drinking man who wants to banish the odor of alcohol. Chewing a cardamom seed is far more effective than Binaca or Listerine. You will not be growing this plant in house or garden, but keep the ancient condiment on your herb-shelf, preferably in whole seed form; though ground cardamom is on the market and is useful. The whole cardamom keeps better. The outer beige pod is tasteless and must be broken open. Within are the pungent dark brown seeds which you can grind yourself in mortar and pestle for maximum flavor. Plant is native to India and belongs to ginger family. Also produced in Guatemala and Ceylon. The king of Babylon grew it in the famous hanging gardens of that city in 721 B.C. Used as medicine, food seasoning, and in perfumes since earliest times. Old Romans prized it, believing its use offset their excesses. Much used in cosmetic industry today. If you have ever been to the great bazaars of the East, a sniff of your bottle of cardamom will waft you back there, for its odor permeates those bustling places. Cardamom provides the magic carpet to a more exotic cuisine, which explains why it's the second most expensive seasoning in the world. Only saffron tops it in price. High Time the American housewife discovered its deliciousness and versatility.

Cardamom in Cooking

Try a dash in apple pie, as the Scandinavians do. It's an interesting switch from cinnamon. Use it in any and all baked goods for subtle new flavor — also in meat loaf, with chicken, and to turn a hamburger from a sow's ear into a silk purse. (½ teaspoon cardamom to 1 pound of meat.) Especially good in fruit cup and gives a really sophisticated touch to after-dinner coffee; also good for the digestion. Your guests won't have to reach for the overadvertised "Di-Gel" when they go home. If you grind your own cardamom, the outer shell that holds the seeds is easily opened by hand. Or use a rolling pin to break shells open. Then crush seeds with small mortar and pestle. To buy the ground cardamom is easier, but just be sure it hasn't been on your herb shelf for years.

Cardamom Coffee (Serves 4)

In after-dinner coffee pot put: 2 tablespoons of instant coffee or Sanka, ¼ teaspoon ground cardamom, 2 cups of boiling water. Stir. Allow to sit a few minutes to develop flavor. Serve in demitasse cups — with sugar only. No cream!

Helen Davidson's Fruit Cup

Fresh fruit with a dash of cardamom, Kirsch for sweetening, and topped with sprigs of mint. M-m-m!

Cardamom Sweet Potatoes (Serves 6)

1 can (17 ounces) sweet potatoes, mashed
4 tablespoons sugar
1 teaspoon vanilla
1/4 teaspoon salt
1/4 teaspoon nutmeg
1/4 teaspoon ground cardamom
} stir into the mashed sweet potatoes, reserving 1 tablespoon of the sugar

1/4 cup milk, mixed into above, thoroughly
3 tablespoons butter, melted. Reserve about 1 tablespoon. Mix the rest into above.

Turn this mixture into a buttered one-quart casserole. Spread on the remaining butter. Sprinkle on the remaining sugar. Bake in 350° oven for about 1/2 hour or until slightly browned.

~~~~~

Betty Lilly's Cardamom Fruit Cup

Combine frozen pineapple chunks with their juice, fresh strawberries, honey, to taste, a little ground cardamom, to taste. Serve from your best glass bowl. (!)

~~~~~

Gladys Elviken's Norwegian Yule Bread

(Makes 2 large or 4 small loaves. A tried and true Norwegian favorite.)

- 1 package dried yeast ⎫ mixed in the cup and allowed to
- ¼ cup of lukewarm water ⎭ rest until yeast softens.
- 2 cups of milk, scalded, and poured into large mixing bowl
- ¼ pound stick of butter (⅓ cup) ⎫ stirred into hot milk and then
- 3 Tablespoons sugar ⎭ allowed to cool.
- 2 teaspoons salt
- 3 eggs, well beaten
- 6½ cups flour (about)
- 1 cup seedless raisins
- 1 cup currants
- 1 cup candied citron
- ½ teaspoon ground cardamom seeds

When hot milk mixture has cooled, add 2 cups of the flour and beat in thoroughly. Then add softened yeast and eggs. Stir in remaining flour, to which fruit and cardamom have been added. Knead until smooth and not sticking to board. Put the kneaded dough back into the mixing bowl, which has been washed and buttered. Let rise until doubled in bulk. Knead down lightly. Shape into 2 or 4 loaves and place in buttered bread pans. Brush with milk. Sprinkle with sugar. Let rise until doubled. Bake in 350° preheated oven, one hour for large loaves, less for small. Watch and judge.   Merry Christmas!

CELERY – The-non-stop-throughout-the-year-all-over-edible-herb

Every part of this marvelous herb is usable: root, stalk, leaf, seed. Native to Southern Europe, it belongs to the carrot family. Wild celery found woven into garlands in Egyptian tombs. Greeks and Romans grew it for medicine rather than food. No wonder! Read on. Believed a remedy for rheumatism, arthritis, neuralgia. Used as carminative, diuretic, to restore appetite, steady the nerves, to treat high blood pressure and failing eyesight, as an antidote to alcoholism. Of course it was and still is considered an aphrodisiac. Ancient intuitiveness concerning celery has, in a sense, been scientifically corroborated today, for it is found to be loaded with vitamins and minerals. By the 17th century celery had been introduced to Europe as a food plant, and the great gardeners of the old world developed it into something almost beyond recognition from its wild cousin. The fat, crunchy stalks of today are the result of their efforts. Celery, as we know it, was first produced in this country by Dutch farmers in Kalamazoo, Michigan, in 1874. Fresh celery juice is served in health food stores today as an all-round tonic. So the circle is complete. We are back to the Greek and Roman idea of celery as a medicine. Celery seed that we buy at the store comes, for the most part, from the wild cousin who lives in Europe and is often called "smallage", not from our fat, green, pascal, domesticated delight. Then there is the herb called <u>lovage</u> which you may grow in your garden if you care to. Our ancestors grew lovage for its celery taste. But they couldn't get <u>our</u> wonderful celery!

Celery in Cooking

A bunch of celery in the refrigerator and celery seed on the herb shelf are basic household supplies like salt and pepper. Never be without them. Celery, in all its forms, makes an excellent substitute for those on salt-free diets. Likewise for the unhappy person who can't tolerate onions. Celery peps up any dish in which it is used, especially celery seed.

Add cut up celery at the last minute to most creamed dishes, in creamed chicken and turkey for sure. It gives as much crunch as water chestnuts and more flavor.

Use celery seed in canapés, dips, bread and rolls, tomato juice, stewed tomatoes, egg dishes, meat loaf, hamburgers, stews, soups, chowders, salad dressing, coleslaw, potato salad, fruit salad, sandwich spreads, vegetables, relishes, pickles and in many fish dishes. In most instances the chopped fresh celery is a pleasant addition.

Of course save outer stalks and leaves for added flavor and nourishment in soups.

Celery stalks filled with seasoned cream cheese or cottage cheese are the first things reached for on the canapé tray.

Be conscientious and scrape the strings off of the larger stalks. They are infinitely more tempting that way — and thereby made as tender as the hearts.

Don't let a day go by without the use of celery!

Texas Celery Seed Salad Dressing (Makes 8 cups)

2¼ cups sugar
4½ teaspoons salt
4 teaspoons paprika
4 teaspoons celery seed
} mixed together by hand in large beater bowl.

1⅝ cups vinegar
1⅓ cups tomato ketchup
1 onion
} run through the blender and added to above.

2 cups salad oil, poured very slowly into the above ingredients, with the beater running.

This dressing keeps indefinitely in refrigerator. Texans have cause to boast when it comes to this recipe!

Betty Spencer's Double-Boiler Celery

Scrape and wash and chop celery into small pieces. (About ½ cup per person) Put in a double-boiler with a lump of butter, a generous sprinkling of celery seed and onion salt, to taste. Cook over boiling water until celery is slightly transparent, but not mushy. Before serving, pour some real cream over all. Heat. Serve in sauce dishes. An elegant vegetable from household staples. Ever so good with game.

Braised Celery Hearts (Serves 6)

<u>3 celery hearts</u>, leaves cut off, cut in half, thoroughly washed. Cook until just barely tender in boiling, salted water containing <u>one onion</u>, <u>one bay leaf</u>. Remove from water, cool, place in buttered, shallow baking dish.

<u>2 beef bouillon cubes</u>
<u>2 cups boiling water</u> } dissolve cubes in water

<u>2 tablespoons butter</u>, melted
<u>2 tablespoons flour</u> } Stir together and then gradually add the above hot bouillon to make a smooth sauce.

Pour the thin brown sauce over the celery, which is ready for the oven at once or hours later, to suit your convenience. Bake at 400° for about 45 minutes. Celery hearts are available in cans — expensive, but worth it, in the interest of speed.

———————

CORIANDER

"And the house of Israel called the name thereof Manna: and it was like coriander seed, white; and the taste was like wafers made with honey." (Exodus 16:31) The word coriander derives from a Greek word meaning "bedbug" — but don't let that "bug you". Only the foliage and unripened seed give off a strange odor. The fully ripe seeds have a delicate, spicy, fragrant aroma, loved by all. There are those who crave the odd-smelling foliage, especially the Orientals, Mexicans and South Americans. It is sometimes called "Chinese parsley," and the Chinese thought it could bestow immortality. Coriander is an annual herb of the parsley family, indigenous to the European-Mediterranean area, and is a cinch to grow almost anywhere. Miraculously, it is not attacked by garden pests. They won't come near it. One of the first herbs grown by American colonists. Much grown in India and used in curry. Used in Egypt for medicine and food. Seeds of coriander found in shops of Pompeii when that city was unearthed. Grew in Hanging Gardens of Babylon, in Charlemagne's gardens. Brought to England by the Romans. Mentioned in "Thousand and One Nights." Used in love potions during Middle Ages. Was associated with fennel in summoning devils. As with caraway, coriander seeds are sometimes sugar-coated to make comfits. Considered a tonic for stomach and heart (½ teaspoon seeds mixed with honey, taken before meals). Recommended as cough medicine, to prevent gout, to take away sounds in ears and the pains of childbirth. Used in medicines today only because of pleasant taste. Makes fragrant toilet water. Used in Chartreuse and other liqueurs, in vermouth, and in gin distilling. Coriander is grown in Kentucky especially for the liquor industry. One of those meat-magic-medicine-good-for-man-or-beast-herbs. Grow it outdoors but don't bother to bring the plants in the house. But be sure the manna-like seeds bless your herb shelf.

Coriander in Cooking

Having grown coriander in your summer garden, try a few of the tender green leaves in salads. I have, — and join with those who like them.

Coriander seed is available whole or ground. Better have both varieties. (You could save your own seeds from herb garden if you care to.) Taste is reminiscent of sage and lemon.

Coriander flavors pastries, cookies, muffins, buns, sausages, frankfurters. Good with meats. Try flavoring custards with it, plus a little grated lemon and orange peel.

Good in sauce for wild game and in poultry stuffing. A sprinkling on roast of pork is recommended.

Adds zip to pickled beets, Scotch broth, rice pudding.

Add seeds to apples, pears, dried fruits while they are cooking.

Add to marinades.

Try adding 1/4 teaspoon of seeds when making soup stock.

Even though the Israelites are on record as having wearied of their manna-like-coriander, there is not a chance that you will tire of the refreshment this herb lends to the various dishes suggested.

Boiled Artichokes (Serves 4)

<u>4 artichokes</u>, trimmed of outer leaves and stalks
<u>boiling salted water</u> — Drop the artichokes therein.
<u>4 coriander seeds</u>) added to above. Simmer, covered,
<u>juice of 1 lemon</u>) about 40 minutes, or until outer leaves pull off easily.

Serve with melted butter or Hollandaise Sauce.

~~~~~~

Coriander Coffee

Crush coriander seeds, one at a time, in smallest mortar and pestle. Place one seed in each coffee cup. Fill with hot coffee. Serve with sugar only. Try it! Remember, it could be a digestive and/or a love potion.

~~~~~~

Coriander Cookies (about 6 dozen)

2 cups flour
1 cup sugar
2 Tablespoons ground coriander seed (!)
} mixed together in mixing bowl

¾ cup soft butter (1½ sticks) - worked into above

1 egg, slightly beaten
1 teaspoon vanilla
1 Tablespoon milk
} stirred together and added to above.

Mix all together thoroughly. Roll into little ½ inch balls. Place on cookie sheet. Flatten each ball with a fork. Bake in preheated 400° oven for 6 to 8 minutes. Watch carefully! Cool on wire rack. Store in airtight container.

~~~~~~~~~~

DILL — to avert the evil eye.

The word "dill" comes from the old Norse "dilla" meaning "to lull". Drink dill tea to overcome insomnia. A native herb of Europe belonging to the parsley family. No garden should be without it both outdoors and indoors. It grows like magic from seed, and is such an accommodating herb that it grows even near the Arctic Circle. A favorite herb of the Russians and their near neighbors. Both seeds and leaves are deliciously edible. Dill was used as a drug by Babylonian and Assyrian doctors. It was cultivated in Palestine and by the Greeks and Romans. Injured knights placed burned dill seeds on their wounds to promote healing. Medieval gardeners could not raise it fast enough for love potions, the casting of spells and for charms against such spells. Carrying a bag of dried dill over the heart insured one against being hexed. Dill, being under Mercury, is alleged to strengthen the brain. Supposed to improve nerves, nails, hair, to quiet colicky babies, to help the flow of mothers' milk, to treat all digestive disorders. Used today, commercially, to scent perfumes, soaps. One ancient source claims that dill "assuageth rumbling in a man's stomach and wicked winds. Also it destroyeth the hiccups." You can't lose with dill in your garden! When it comes to flavor, dill has no substitutes; it stands alone, is utterly unique.

Dill in Cooking

Fresh chopped dill leaves, dried dill or dill seeds enhance all cold vegetable salads as well as shellfish salads, especially shrimp.

Basis of many pickles and of dill vinegar.

Great as a touch in the green salad bowl and as a garnish to the fish platter, especially salmon.

Dill leaves make as lovely a garnish on almost everything as does the ubiquitous parsley. Use it in place of parsley now and then for a refreshing change.

Use seeds or chopped leaves (sparingly - the flavor grows) in creamed chicken, over steaks and chops, even in apple pie.

Great in sour cream (or yogurt) sauce for cucumbers. Dill and cucumbers go hand in glove.

Use with sauerkraut, green beans, beets, broccoli, cauliflower, soups, stews, tomato juice, and in cottage and cream cheese.

Especially good with deviled eggs.

Try a green salad richly endowed with slightly cooked green beans, thin red onion rings, and a sprinkling of chopped fresh dill.

Dill Dip (Serves 20)

- 2/3 cup salad dressing
- 2/3 cup sour cream
- 1 Tablespoon minced onion
- 1 Tablespoon parsley flakes
- 1 Tablespoon dill seed
- 1 teaspoon salt

Mix in order given and serve with assorted chilled vegetable sticks: carrot, celery, cucumber, cauliflower, white turnip, green pepper, whatever.

You may substitute fresh chopped dill leaves and parsley if available. In any event let the Dill Dip season for a while in the refrigerator. The dill taste strengthens with Time.

~~~~~~~~~~

Dill-icious Cabbage Salad (Serves 8)

4 cups finely-shredded cabbage
1 cup diced celery
¼ cup chopped parsley
½ cup sour cream
1 Tablespoon chopped onion
1½ teaspoons dill seed
½ teaspoon salt
pepper, a sprinkling, freshly ground
2 teaspoons lemon juice

green pepper rings, reserved for garnish

Combine all ingredients, except the green pepper, in order given. Toss lightly; decorate with thinly sliced rings of green pepper.

You think cabbage indigestible? Dill is ever so popular in Europe, with both cabbage and cucumbers, not only for its flavor, but because dill acts as a digestive.

~~~~~~~~~~

FENNEL

"**The Meetin' Seed**" it has been called because the Puritans were prone to chew it during the endless church services of their era. Fennel has the scent of "new mown hay" from which it takes its name. Also called "The Fish Herb" and "Florence Fennel." Fennel is closely related to dill and cross-pollinates with same, so watch out and plant far from dill or the resultant seed will have a dull, miscellaneous flavor. A hardy perennial of the parsley family. Easily grown outdoors and in. Popular with Egyptians, Romans, Greeks. Greeks believed it induced longevity, strength, courage. Pliny, in first century, noted that snakes, casting off their skins, ate fennel to renew their sight. Therefore used for eye troubles. Chinese and Hindus used it as snake bite remedy. Used in Northern Europe for 900 years. Ancient Saxons believed in nine sacred herbs (of which fennel was one) with power to combat diseases, which were also supposed to be nine in number. Fennel much used in witchcraft. Both Milton and Longfellow wrote of its sweet scent. Considered a digestive, tonic, laxative, an aid in expelling poisons from blood. Good for bites, kidneys, lungs, liver, jaundice, and an aid in producing mothers' milk. But probably most important: "Used for those that are grown fat, to cause them to grow more gaunt and lank."

From "The Goblet of Life" by Longfellow:

"Above the lowly plants it towers,
The fennel, with its yellow flowers,
And in an earlier age than ours
Was gifted with the wondrous powers,
Lost vision to restore.
It gave new strength, and fearless mood;
And gladiators, fierce and rude,
Mingled it in their daily food;
And he who battled and subdued,
A wreath of fennel wore."

Fennel in Cooking

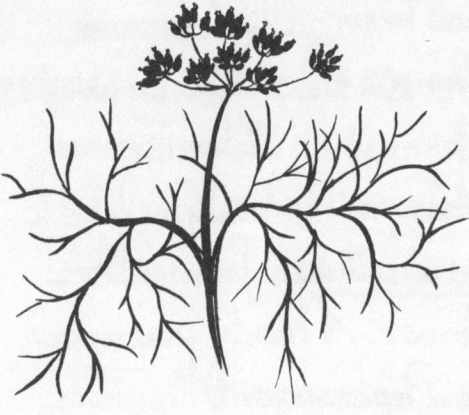

As with celery, all parts are edible: roots, stalks, leaves, seeds.

Make fennel seed tea for relief of indigestion. (See back of booklet.)

Use the fresh leaves in green salad bowl.

The seeds make fine seasoning for baked goods. Sprinkle on breads, rolls, cakes, cookies, before baking.

Put a few seeds in apple pie and baked apple.

Meats and poultry: scatter a few seeds in pan when roasting, in water when stewing.

Add seeds to sauerkraut while heating it.

Use a tiny bit of seed in salad dressing.

Above all remember that this is <u>the fish herb</u> and has a great affinity for any fish dish, hot or cold. Use seeds or fresh green leaves, roots, whatever. If your fish dish has a faint suggestion of fennel it will be a success.

Scatter a few fennel seeds in crumb topping for any seafood casserole.

Fennel Potatoes (serves 6)

5 medium potatoes, boiled in jackets
2 teaspoons finely chopped fennel leaves
   (or 1 teaspoon crushed seeds)
4 tablespoons butter (reserve 2 tablespoons)
1/3 cup milk
Salt and freshly ground pepper to taste

1 egg   ⎫
1/4 cup milk ⎬ beaten together
            ⎭
paprika

Peel potatoes while still hot, and mash well. Stir in fennel, only 2 tablespoons of the butter, milk, salt and pepper. Place this in a buttered casserole of appropriate size. Spread egg-and-milk mixture over the top. Dot with the remaining 2 tablespoons of butter. Sprinkle with paprika. A great potato dish, not only because of its unique flavor, but because it may be prepared in the morning for an evening meal. Bake, uncovered, in preheated 350° oven until hot, and browned on top.

Fennel Seed Cookies (makes about 4 dozen)

½ cup soft butter (1 stick)
1 teaspoon fennel seed, crushed
¼ teaspoon salt
1 cup sugar
} Cream together well.

1 egg, well beaten, and stirred into above.

1 ¾ cups flour
1 ½ teaspoons baking powder
} mixed together and stirred into above.

Refrigerate the batter for 2 hours.

Roll into one-inch balls.

Place on lightly buttered cookie sheet.

Press flat with a fork.

Bake in preheated 375° oven for about 10 minutes, but watch carefully.
Cool on wire racks. Store in airtight container.

LEMON

LEMON could have been what Eve handed Adam in the Garden. It is certainly knowledgeable to make constant use of lemon in food preparation and it's hard to think of anything better to be growing on the tree of knowledge. Lemons were once called "Persian Apples," so the claim about Eden may have validity. To include lemon in a book of herbs may seem odd, but in the wider sense it _is_ an herb and one of the world's oldest and best of seasonings. Lemon trees were usually a part of medieval herb gardens, potted in colder climates so as to be brought indoors. A household without fresh lemons at hand is unthinkable. The plastic substitute is beneath discussion. Lemons were first noted in 4000 B.C. in what is now Pakistan. The seeds have been scattered around the world as fast as man's explorations. Columbus brought lemon seed to the Western Hemisphere on his second voyage in 1493, a feat for which he is not given sufficient recognition. It is a year-round crop in the U.S.A. now and the most used. The first Queen Elizabeth's favorite tipple, and that of the Vikings before her, was Mead made of lemons, honey, water, spices, herbs. This concoction was allowed to stand three months and then bottled. Lemons' medicinal properties are many, doubtless because they are loaded with vitamin C. They prevent scurvy, colds, treat fevers, cleanse the blood. Helpful in cases of jaundice, pulmonary and skin ailments. Lemon cream for the face is still around. It is much used in soaps and various cosmetics both for its bleaching propensities and its fragrance. Lemon is the great purifier and whitener. Rust stains were removed with lemon in the old days, (not to mention freckles). Why not try growing a dwarf variety of lemon tree in your indoor herb garden, and establish a little Eden of your own?

Lemon in Cooking

When choosing lemons at the market, pick the heaviest ones.

Keep them in plastic bag in refrigerator.

Cut off or grate off only the thin, yellow, outer skin when using the rind. The precious oil and flavor is in this part. The white inner part of rind is bitter.

Almost any drink is improved by a thin sliver of the yellow rind, twisted, and rubbed around edge of glass.

There is no meal that is not improved by the use of lemon at some point, be it the juice squeezed over a shellfish cocktail at the beginning or a lemon pie, that makes use of both juice and grated rind, as a triumphal ending.

Fish in any form is almost unthinkable without lemon, even to lemon in the finger bowl after lobster.

German Meat Balls owe their authority to the use of lemon.

Never put a leg of lamb into the oven without a nice shower of lemon juice

Try a bit of lemon over boiled potatoes and give them the Lebanese touch.

Put grated lemon peel or extract or juice into breads, cakes, cookies, custards, rice pudding — and in many fruits for added zip.

A hot lemon toddy at bedtime will often ward off an oncoming cold.

Greek Soup (Serves 6)

<u>6 cups chicken broth</u>, canned or your own.
<u>1/3 cup real rice</u>, stirred into above and simmered for 1/2 hour, or until rice is tender
<u>2 egg yolks</u>
<u>juice of one lemon</u> } well beaten together

Add 1 cup of the hot, cooked broth very gradually to egg-lemon mixture. Then pour this back into the rest of the soup, stirring constantly. Heat for a minute, but do not let it boil! Correct for salt if need be. Serve at once. You may make a similar soup with broth from a lamb bone. The latter is really more "Greek." Both soups are excellent under any conditions, but very reviving if one is feeling a bit frail.

~~~~~~~~~~

Favorite Baked Chicken (Serves 2)

Place the parts of one cut-up frying <u>chicken</u> in a buttered, shallow baking dish. Paint them with melted <u>butter</u>. Anoint all <u>generously</u> with <u>lemon juice</u>. <u>Salt it</u>. Bake it in 375° oven for an hour or more, until crisp. The simplicity of this dish is <u>exceeded</u> only by its deliciousness. Lemon is the <u>reason</u>.

~~~~~~~~~~

Gladys Elviken's Lemon-Carrot Relish

<u>1 bunch (or package) carrots</u> }
<u>1 lemon, seeds removed</u> } put through grinder
<u>1 cup sugar</u>, stirred into above

Store in refrigerator. This will pep up any meal — color-wise, taste-wise.

Lemon-ginger Fruit (to go with meat)

<u>1 can pear halves</u> (1 pound, 14 ounces) <u>with the syrup</u>
<u>1 can apricot halves</u>   "   "   , drained
<u>3 tablespoons chopped, crystalized ginger</u>
<u>5 very thin slices of lemon, quartered</u>

Butter a 2 quart casserole. Mix pears and juice, drained apricots, and ginger, therein. Tuck in the lemon slices, in any pattern that suits your mood. Bake, uncovered, in 325° oven for a half hour. Serve very hot or very cold. Good with any meat, but especially ham.

MARJORAM

means "joy of the mountain" and symbolizes blushes, happiness, honor. Brides and grooms wore wreaths of marjoram throughout Europe, where it was spread far and wide by conquering Romans. Native to the Mediterranean area, it has been newly classified by botanists as *Majorana hortensis* which is the true marjoram offered by the seed houses as "sweet marjoram." This finally clears up an age-old confusion between marjoram and oregano. It seems there is a wild marjoram in Europe which is really oregano. Our wild marjoram is not, and is considered useless. Majorana hortensis is a perennial, but best treated as an annual, for it is so easily raised from seed. Grow it outdoors and indoors. It is one of the great herbs of the mint family. There is an old saying for new cooks: "When in doubt use marjoram." It was loved by the ancient Egyptians. The Greeks used it to cure narcotic poisoning, convulsions, dropsy. It was a must in every medieval garden. People loved its "noble taste" and its beauty as a border plant. A favorite strewing herb and air sweetener. "The Strewer of Herbs in Ordinary" to James II of England, in the mid 17th Century, scattered eighteen bushels of marjoram and sweet herbs at James' coronation. Spanish peasants consider any salad incomplete without it. Marjoram once took the place of hops in the brewing of ale and beer. Used in water for bathing and for handwashing at meals. Bound upon the head for colds, headaches. An internal-external cure-all. A breath sweetener, a charm against witchcraft. "Maketh joints supple and helpeth the loss of speech by resolution of the tongue." Used in perfumes long ago — and now. Used as flavoring for tobacco and even in furniture polish. Well named "joy of the mountain."

Marjoram in Cooking

"Indeed, sir, she was the sweet marjoram of the salad, or, rather the herb of grace." (Shakespeare) Marjoram <u>is</u> an herb of grace in salads. Try it.

Use marjoram fresh or dried; but, of course, the fresh is best. It is called "the herb of 1000 uses" in the modern kitchen.

Tense? Try marjoram tea: "Warms the stomach, aids digestion." Sweeten with honey. An excellent sedative nightcap. The English make tea from it a great deal. (See back of booklet.)

Lends enticing flavor to all meats, fish, game, eggs, and about every vegetable one can name. Put a pinch in cooking water of vegetables. ¼ to ½ teaspoon of dried marjoram to about six servings is the rule. If you use it fresh from the garden you may increase this amount. But always with herbs: better too little than too much.

An excellent addition to poultry stuffing.

Makes interesting jelly. (See back of booklet.)

Crab Meat Entrée
(Serves 3 or 4)

<u>1 can very best crabmeat, flaked
1 can mushroom soup
juice of ½ lemon
¼ teaspoon dried marjoram</u>

Combine above ingredients in top of double boiler. Heat. Serve on <u>Melba Toast</u>.

A ready-in-a-jiffy luncheon dish.

Quickie Spinach with Marjoram
(Serves 6 to 8)

- 2 packages frozen, thawed, chopped spinach
- 1 package onion soup mix
- 1 cup sour cream
- ½ teaspoon dried marjoram (or double the amount if fresh)

Mix all of above ingredients together.
Place in buttered baking dish.
Bake in 325° oven until bubbling hot.

~~~~~~~~

Marinated Green Beans with Marjoram (Serves 6 to 8)

- 2 (nine-ounce) packages frozen green beans, slightly cooked until tender-crisp. Drain. Cool.
- 6 tablespoons salad oil
- 2 tablespoons vinegar
- 2 teaspoons dried marjoram, well crumbled (more if fresh)
- 1 teaspoon sugar
- ½ teaspoon salt
- ¼ teaspoon freshly ground black pepper

Well blended together and poured over beans. Cover and marinate in refrigerator at least 12 hours.

MINT

— symbol of hospitality and wisdom. "The very smell of it reanimates the spirit," Pliny tells us. Sometimes called "Lamb Mint" or "Garden Mint." Mint was once the nymph, Mentha, who attracted the roving eye of Pluto. Pluto's wife, in a jealous frenzy, knocked her down and was in the process of trampling her to death when, presto, Pluto appeared and turned Mentha into a delightful herb — ever sacred to him. We are talking of the best mint, the gourmets' mint: _Mentha spicata_ or spearmint. Grow any others you care to, (There are some 40 varieties!) but why bother with less than the best? Spearmint is much older than peppermint, which wasn't around until about 1700. Ancient Hebrews scattered mint on synagogue floors. Each footstep wafted fragrance. Jesus said, "Woe unto you, scribes and Pharisees, hypocrites! for ye tithe of mint and anise and cummin, and have omitted the weightier matters of the law, judgement, mercy and faith." Mint is native to Egypt and the Holy Land and is used copiously by the Moslem Arabs today in their tall glasses of hot, sweet tea strongly laced with chopped mint. Moslems, not being wine drinkers, make mint tea important socially; and, too, there is firm belief in its aphrodisiac qualities. Mint is supposed to soothe as well as excite, which sounds ambivalent, but that's the story. It induces sleep, clears the sinuses (think of all the menthol remedies in a modern drug store!), helps digestion, rheumatism, hiccups, stings, flatulence, and "clears the voice before an oration." Taken wherever Roman soldiers went. Brought home by Crusaders. Pilgrims brought mint to New England. Ancient Greeks and Romans rubbed tables with mint before guests arrived. Hot countries still have bunches hung in doorways for breeze to blow through. Grow it outdoors, indoors, and buy _plants_, not seeds. Needs little sun, benefits from frequent cutting. There are few plants as loved and useful. Mint will take over a whole garden, so show your love by disciplining it. It keeps mice away! Try it in lieu of traps or poison.

Mint in Cooking

Mint jelly to go with lamb is delicious but certainly overused. Try other tricks such as those in following recipes. Mint is the "lamb herb" and should be served with it in some form. Don't forget old fashioned, "bitey" mint sauce with vinegar.

Put a pinch of mint in lamb stew.

Use it in pea soup. It not only enriches the flavor but counteracts the tendency of peas to produce gas.

Use in fish sauces, fruit cup, sprinkled over bland vegetables. Use a bit in French Dressing, in cabbage salad.

Make hot mint tea, as the Arabs do, loading the tea with chopped mint. Ditto for iced tea.

For a luncheon party on a hot day, fold a stalk of mint in the napkin. (Decorative and refreshing).

And, of course, make some mint jelly.

Serve plain mint tea. (See back of booklet.)

Minted Peas (Serves 4)

- 1 package frozen peas (get the fancy petits pois if you're in extravagant mood.)
- 1 generous tablespoon butter
- 1 teaspoon sugar
- ¼ cup water
- salt – a light sprinkling

Put all this in pan on medium burner, covered. Bring to a boil and simmer just until peas separate – no longer!

- 1 tablespoon fresh, chopped spearmint (or ½ teaspoon dried mint)
- 1 teaspoon grated lemon peel

mixed into above when removed from burner.

This may all be done the morning of a party. Let the partially cooked peas cool; then cover and forget them. Just before serving, bring to a rapid boil and boil no longer than 3 to 5 minutes. Do not pour off the good juices if any are left. Put a dab of butter on top and serve with slotted spoon. These are what I call company-ready peas. You may do it all at last minute if you care to. Serve with roast lamb, and do not repeat the mint theme. That would be redundant.

Minted Pears

1 can pear halves (1 pound 14 ounces)
1 Tablespoon mint flakes
   (or 2 tablespoons fresh chopped spearmint)

Drain juice from pears.
Add mint to the juice and simmer for 10 minutes.
Remove from stove and add a little green
      vegetable coloring to the juice.
Pour the hot, green juice over the pears.
      You may strain the juice or not.
      It will be of stronger mint flavor
      if flecks of mint are retained.
      Suit your own taste.
Refrigerate. Serve with lamb in your
best glass dish, in place of mint jelly.

~~~~~~~~~~~

MUSTARD

"A tale without love is like beef without mustard: an insipid dish." (Anatole France) King Louis XI of France was so fearful his hosts might not serve mustard that he always carried the royal mustard pot with him. The world has taken a tip from Louis for it consumes 400 million pounds of mustard annually. In the U.S. more mustard is consumed than any other seasoning except pepper, somewhat due to the hot dog, no doubt. Unique among herbs: when dry it seems as bland as cornstarch; mixed with water — wow! Of Asiatic origin — the Chinese adore it. It has been in use since prehistoric times. Jesus said, "The kingdom of heaven is like to a grain of mustard seed.... which indeed is the least of all seeds, but when it is grown it is the greatest among herbs." Of course the Roman soldiers spread it about and Charlemagne grew it. The word <u>mustard</u> derives from the Latin <u>mustum</u> or <u>must</u>, the expressed juice of grape or other fruit which was mixed with ground mustard seeds. There is both black and white mustard seed. The dry mustard we buy is the ground seed of both. The commercial mustard <u>seeds</u> are from the White mustard plant. The White mustard produces foliage much prized as a salad and potherb. Grow some for salad purposes if you care to, but the seeds are so easily purchased that it is hardly worth growing the herb for seed purposes. Mustard has been used for medicine, condiment, food, for countless ages. An herb of Mars, to use both externally and internally. Good for scorpion bites, coughs, epilepsy and to quicken dull spirits; helps poor appetite, flatulence, bad breath, colds, catarrh, pneumonia, arthritic pain; is a sterilizing agent, deodorant, antiseptic, laxative. Anything so all-healing would have to have another side to the coin. Used in large quantities in the dread mustard gas of war, it is lethal. Interesting it should have been thought to be under Mars, symbolic of god of war, ages before modern man dreamed up such deadly and warlike use of mustard.

Mustard in Cooking

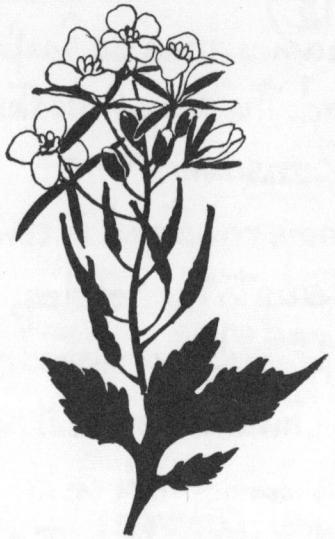

No mystery about mustard for it is one herb with which everyone is familiar. However, it acts mysteriously: mixed with water it "ripens" in about 15 minutes and is at its best. One should throw out what is left after the meal for aroma and taste fade fast. If you want a hot mustard sauce to last, add vinegar.

Mustard added to mayonnaise, curries, or salad dressings acts as a preservative.

Whole mustard seed is used in many pickles, in pickled meat and fish.

Dry mustard improves meats, sauces, gravies, all sorts of egg dishes and cheese dishes.

Add ½ teaspoon mustard seed to cooking water for broccoli, Brussels sprouts and cabbage. Add to sauerkraut before cooking. Add a few seeds to coleslaw.

Prepared mustard, which is a blend of vinegar and various spices, is so popular for so many things (hot dogs, ham, sandwich fillings of all kinds) that most kitchen cupboards boast too many jars of mustard in varying states of staleness. Its antiseptic quality seems to cause it to last forever.

Piping Pigs (Appetizer for 12)

<u>1 package best hot dogs</u> (1 pound or 10 hot dogs) cut into bite-sized pieces.

<u>1 cup prepared mustard</u> } thoroughly mixed
<u>1 cup red currant jelly</u> } together and poured over hot dogs, which have been placed in stove-to-table dish.

Place in 300° oven and bake until bubbling hot, covered. Serve with tooth picks. May be kept warm over candle warmer or hot tray, but chances are they will disappear too fast to bother. (Baking time about ½ hour.)

~~~~~~~~

Sister Bet's Hot Mustard

2 Tablespoons dry mustard } mixed
2 tablespoons vinegar

1 teaspoon sugar
¼ teaspoon salt } mixed
1 tablespoon oil

Put the two mixtures together. Mix well. Authoritative!

~~~~~~~~

Mary Stone's Mustard Sauce

4 tablespoons dry mustard
2 tablespoons sugar
½ tablespoon salt
2 eggs, well beaten
4 tablespoons vinegar
2 tablespoons cold water

Mix all together in top of double boiler, in order given. Cook over hot water, stirring constantly, until it just begins to thicken. No more!

1 tablespoon butter, stirred into hot sauce when it is removed from stove. Cool.

1 cup cream, whipped and added to above cooled sauce. Fold in lightly.

This elegant sauce turns any meal into an EVENT. Thank you, Mary!

~~~~~~~~~~~~~~~~

ONION — "rose among roots," of the lily family and known to history for more than 4000 years. Onions were deified in Egypt for Pliny tells us, "Onions and garlic are among the Gods of Egypt and by these they make their oaths." Because of sheaths enveloping bulb it suggested symbol of universe to Egyptians. Garlic bulb found in King Tut's tomb. The Great Pyramid at Cheops had an inscription saying that 1600 talents of silver had been spent on onions for the workmen. These same workmen, the Israelites, sulked and salivated on their desert sojourn, nostalgically remembering the onions of Egypt, the discomforts of slavery forgotten. Unlike the Egyptians and Israelites, the people of ancient India abhorred garlic and onions. They were "forbidden fruit" in some areas and people who insisted upon eating them had to go out of town to do so! Garlic was the common food of the Roman laborer, but the upper classes disdained it as a sign of vulgarity. Garlic and onions arrived in England via the conquering Romans, in the New World via Columbus. Then Columbus changed the culinary habits of the Old World by bringing back potatoes and tomatoes. An interesting switch, enriching both sides of the world. Henry IV of France "cracked garlic cloves in his teeth and had a breath that could fell an ox at 20 paces." He should have eaten some parsley, which kills garlic and onion breath. Message from Gen. U.S. Grant: "I will not move my army without onions." Three carloads were shipped at once. Recognized as cure for scurvy long before modern science found onions rich in minerals and vitamins. Folk medicine claims onions are a cure-all. Fresh cut onions used in sickroom during plague apparently prevented spread of disease; some areas of modern research investigating the claim. Used in witchcraft, counter witchcraft. "The juice [of onion] upon a bald head in the sunne, bringing the hair again very speedily." Still used as cold remedy externally and internally, as diuretic, soporific, wart and burn remedy. British army used garlic juice to treat battle wounds as recently as World War I.

Onion in Cooking

"This is every cook's opinion —
No savory dish without an onion,
But lest your kissing should be spoiled
Your onions must be fully boiled." (Jonathan Swift)

"Put onions in everything but ice cream." (Sister Bet)

The above quotes say all. Have braided strings of the red Spanish onions, bowls of regular onions, jars of garlic, the various handy dried and powdered varieties of everything in the onion family — and, of course, fresh chives growing on a sunny window sill in your kitchen. They serve for decoration, food, flavoring. Use them all — all day, every day. They <u>do</u> improve everything but ice cream, and your health as well.

When making soup stock, to which onion is always added, don't bother to peel. Just wash, cut in half and pop into the soup kettle.

Irish Champ (Serves 6)

(Given me by Miss Rita Eccles, who is straight from the Emerald Isle.)

<u>6 potatoes</u>, peeled
<u>1 cup milk</u>
<u>1 bunch of scallions</u> or 1 generous onion, chopped fine
<u>butter</u>
<u>Salt and freshly ground pepper</u>, to taste

Boil the potatoes, and while they are boiling, bring the milk, the scallions or onion, and a generous piece of butter to a simmer in a separate pan. Let simmer 10 or 15 minutes, no more. When potatoes are cooked, mash them and stir in the hot milk mixture. Season with salt and pepper. No wonder the Irish love potatoes! (Use scallions, if possible. The green enhances the appearance as well as the taste. Chop about halfway up the stem, and discard the rest.)

Basic Baked Onions

My favorite quick and easy way with onions is to wrap them individually in foil; no peeling, no seasoning. Place in a pie plate or any shallow baking dish (in case the juices leak), and bake an hour or even two hours. Baking time depends on size of onions and what happens to be in the oven. Serve in the foil, and let the ones who dine do the rest. When cut open they are sweet as honey, tender, digestible. Each individual may add butter and salt at the table, according to taste. Actually they are totally delicious with nothing added.

Give onions the same treatment on an outdoor grill.

~~~~~~

OREGANO
— the herb of sudden fame, "the pizza herb." Before World War II oregano was never mentioned in records of U.S. customs. Then our soldiers went to Italy and the pizza craze was on. Always indispensable in Italian, Spanish, and South American kitchens, suddenly it hit the herb shelves of the U.S.A. The sale of oregano has increased 5000% since the war! Whatever it is botanically (we touched on that under marjoram), it is a great herb, unique in its own right, stronger than marjoram in flavor and to be used with discretion. It is pronounced <u>or-AY-gano</u>, is a hardy perennial of the mint family. It is easily grown from seed, so have it for salad greens in summer and in winter, too, for it grows well in the house. Native to the hillsides of the Mediterranean region, it has had much the same history as many of the other herbs: spread by the Romans, brought to the New World by early settlers. Physicians of the classical era listed it as a cure for almost every ailment known to man, even coronary conditions. At present its use is limited to the culinary field; but who knows? maybe the ancients knew things that we don't. "Good against wambling of the stomacke," they said ... and "scarcely a better herb growing for relieving loss of appetite."

Oregano in Cooking

The pizza herb, the tomato herb, the essential ingredient of chili powder. Potent. Use sparingly. Aside from all tomato dishes, try a touch in cheese and egg dishes.

Good in bread stuffing for fish.

Gives zip to clear vegetable and beef broths.

Goes with all meats, salads, sauces.

Make an herb butter by adding chopped oregano to heated butter, and pour over cooked onions, peas, spinach, green beans, potatoes, or corn.

Fresh oregano leaves enhance the salad bowl.

Use oregano and basil together, say some authorities. They like each other.

The dried oregano from Greece is best, so find a store that carries it.

Broccoli Soup (Serves 4)

1 package frozen broccoli (10 ounces) cooked in very little water. Do not drain.
1½ cups milk
1 slice of onion
¼ teaspoon oregano
¾ teaspoon curry powder
1 Tablespoon lemon juice
Salt and freshly ground pepper, to taste
2 teaspoons cornstarch

Blend all of above ingredients in blender. Pour into double boiler.

3 tablespoons of butter, added to above.

Cook over hot water stirring constantly. When hot and slightly thickened, serve at once.

Jeanette Russell's Pickled Garden Relish (Serves 10)

½ head cauliflower, cut into flowerets and sliced fairly small
2 carrots, scraped, and cut into thin strips about 2 inches long
1 cup chopped celery
1 green pepper cut into small strips
1 jar pimento (4 ounce size) drained, cut into small strips
1 jar small stuffed olives, green. Coarsely chopped ripe olives may be substituted.
¾ cup vinegar
½ cup salad oil
2 tablespoons sugar
1 teaspoon salt
¼ teaspoon freshly ground pepper
½ teaspoon dried oregano (or 2 teaspoons chopped fresh)

Combine all above ingredients in proper-sized pan. Add ¼ cup water. Bring to a boil, stirring the while. Cover, and simmer just 5 minutes. Cool; then refrigerate 24 hours. Drain before serving.

This dish is a real prize. Difficult to share it, but if Jeanette was generous — I must be.

PARSLEY

— symbolic of mirth, joy, festivity, honor. Horses are said to accelerate speed after nipping parsley and so will you! Has been cultivated for thousands of years, its early history lost in Greek mythology. It is a biennial of the carrot family, but best treated as an annual. There is both curly and the flatter-leaved Italian variety. Grow both in your garden and make lush, wondrous borders of it grown from seed. The seed germinates slowly and for this reason parsley was an object of superstition during the Middle Ages when it was believed the seed had to take time to go down to the devil and come up again before it would begin to grow. The Greeks crowned their heroes with it, but, strangely enough, did not eat it. They decorated tombs with it and the expression "to be in need of parsley" meant one was dead. The Romans, on the other hand, ate it, decorated their best dining halls with it, made crowns of it for diners to wear, believing it prevented drunkenness. It was eaten after banquets to sweeten the breath, showing that our 20th century use of chlorophyll is not new. The stems were once used for green dye. Parsley has even been prescribed to cure sick fish in ponds. Parsley tea indicated for kidney disorders. Parsley will fasten loose teeth, brighten dim eyes, and relieve a stitch in the side. "Beneficial for diabetics, prostate trouble, night blindness, <u>jaded cerebral cells</u>". Good for rheumatism and an aid to digestion; a blood cleanser, a tonic. Especially good for cystitis. In England, where they went so far as to make parsley pie, it takes the place of the stork. "Where did I come from, Mommy?" asks an English child. "From the parsley bed, my dear," was the old reply. Some modern herbalists suggest that those with a family history of cancer should eat all the parsley possible. Keep a pot of parsley in your window in winter for beauty and garnishing purposes, but augment it with many bunches per week purchased at market, for eating.

Parsley in Cooking

A U.S. catering service recently conducted a survey and discovered that over 90% of parsley served as a garnish was left untouched. What a waste! One half cup of chopped parsley supplies 10,000 units of vitamin A alone, not to mention heavy doses of C, iodine, iron, and other life-giving properties. Only parsley is found in both French standbys: <u>bouquet garni</u> and <u>fines herbes</u>. This ultra valuable herb should be a staple in our daily diet and thought of as a food, not a garnish. It is a truly universal herb and should be used as comprehensively as the onion. It has both eye and taste appeal unequalled. Add it, chopped, to all vegetables, meats, fish. My favorite trick is to include copious quantities of it in baking powder biscuits which I serve with various stews. I use the same recipe as a crust for meat pies. Once, on St. Patrick's day, I mixed an extra supply of chopped fresh parsley <u>in</u> the mashed potatoes instead of sprinkling on top. They were not only a festive green but became a family favorite. Two of the best recipes I have follow, suggesting further uses of parsley as a food. You will think up others. Eat parsley and LIVE.

Marion Wing's Parsley Spread
(There are no words to express how much I prize this recipe.)

<u>1 or 2 LARGE bunches of parsley</u> (depending on number of guests), chopped fine after washing and drying well. Use leaves only, not stems.

<u>Mayonnaise or Miracle Whip</u>, mixed with parsley in sufficient quantity to be nicely spreadable, no more.

<u>Salt and freshly ground pepper</u>, to taste

<u>Grated onion</u> (very little, about 1 tablespoon per bunch of parsley)

Chop the parsley well with a good sharp chef's knive. Remember that chopping reduces the parsley greatly. You will soon learn to judge how much to use. The finer chopped the better. (Parsley grinders are an abomination; snipping with scissors is futile.) The knife technique is a cinch, with a little practice. Don't let the simplicity of this recipe put you off. Guests wolf it down with startled delight. Serve it in a small bowl surrounded by Wheat Thins, melba toast, sesame crackers, or Triscuits. This is likewise an excellent spread for dainty tea sandwiches. Used in place of lettuce and mayonnaise in a chicken sandwich, it is sensational. Parsley is an herb with an imposing list of curative virtues: "Good against the stone or torments of the guts," says one old authority. It is reputed to be under the dominion of Mercury and is "very comfortable to the stomach."…. "A medicine nurses give to children with wind in the belly…. Effectual against the venom of any poisonous creature." HAPPY COCKTAIL HOUR!

Parsley Soup (Serves 4)

<u>2 potatoes</u>, cut up
<u>2 onions</u>, cut up
<u>generous dab of butter</u>
<u>very little water</u>
} Simmer until vegetables are cooked. Do not drain. Put in blender.

<u>1 bunch parsley</u>, well washed, stems removed.
    Add to vegetables in blender.

<u>1 can chicken broth</u>, or equivalent of home-made broth.
    Add to blender.

<u>Salt and freshly ground pepper</u>
<u>Curry powder</u>, just a pinch
<u>Worcestershire Sauce</u>, just a sprinkle
} Added to blender. Blend all well.

<u>2 cups of milk</u> (or half cream, half milk)
    Pour into a double boiler and stir in contents of blender. Correct seasoning. Heat and serve with chowder crackers, split, buttered, and baked long, and at low temperature. Or serve with croutons. Garnish soup with chopped fresh chives, if available.

~~~~~~~~~~

In the spring of the year, substitute tender dandelion greens for the parsley! Delicious.

~~~~~~~~~~

PEPPER - The Master Spice

It may seem odd to tuck pepper into an herb book, but it is so important and so casually used today that some facts about it need airing. Also, in the wider sense, it is an herb: the berries from a vine that grows in hot jungle lands that are never farther than 20 degrees from the Equator. Pepper is distributed throughout the world today, and is cheap, considering its exotic past and its importance. The history of the spice/herb trade is, above all, the history of pepper. It was moving westward from India 4000 years ago. Often used in trading as a substitute for money. One peppercorn dropped on the floor was hunted as if it were a lost pearl. When Alaric, king of the Visigoths, besieged Rome in 408 A.D., a major part of the tribute he exacted from the city was 30,000 pounds of pepper. Another source says 3000 pounds — anyway, a lot of pepper. Pepper was much used by ancient Greeks and Romans and considered a carminative, stimulant, aphrodisiac, and cure for diarrhea, cholera, arthritis. Spice merchants were known as "pepperers" in the Middle Ages and the economy of the cities of Alexandria, Genoa, Venice depended on the pepper trade. Taxes, tributes, dowries, and rents were often paid in pepper. In France one pound of pepper could buy a serf his freedom. The finest pepper in the world is called <u>Tellicherry</u>, and since it is no longer priceless, why not use the best? It comes chiefly from the Northern Malabar Coast. <u>Black pepper</u> is made of the whole berry which is picked before ripening and is pickled. <u>White pepper</u> is from ripened berries with the outer covering removed. In the U.S. we use 12 times as much black as white pepper. In Europe the reverse is true. Black is more pungent than white. I find the latter a refinement too great to bother with, though this remark would make the true gourmet shudder. The main thing is to have plenty of pepper mills so as to always have fresh-ground pepper.

Pepper in Cooking

First of all, make up your mind to be the last of the great spenders and equip yourself with an array of pepper grinders: large ones for the kitchen, smaller ones for the dining table. Then buy the best Tellicherry peppercorns and your reputation as a gourmet will be unassailable.

Remember that whole peppercorns keep many years without loss of quality, whereas pre-ground pepper has a short shelf life and is made from the poorest peppercorns. Also, fresh ground pepper will not make you sneeze!

Pepper improves almost everything, even desserts. Grind a little into Pumpkin Pie. It is an important ingredient of Vermont's famous Maple Syrup Pie. (Recipe follows.) It gives a mysterious delectable bouquet and offsets oversweetness.

Why pepper's universal supremacy and popularity? The late Louis Diat, master chef, said that no other seasoning can do so much for so many different types of food. It is often used three times in one dish: cooked with the food, again added when seasoning is corrected, and again at table.

Warning: Pepper cooked in food too long will sometimes turn bitter. It is best to add pepper toward the last, which is true of most herbs.

Veal Scallopine (Serves 6)

2 pounds veal cutlets
salt, freshly ground pepper, flour — placed in paper bag. Put cutlets in the bag and shake gently back and forth until cutlets are coated.

1/4 cup butter and a little splash of salad oil, heated in a large skillet. Brown the veal quickly in this. Remove from heat.

1/2 pound fresh mushrooms, sliced, and spread over meat.

1 cup dry white wine
1 large onion, sliced
1 tablespoon sugar
1 parsley sprig
1/4 teaspoon rosemary
1/4 teaspoon marjoram
1/4 teaspoon peppercorns

} blended in blender and poured over meat and mushrooms.

Cover tightly, and simmer until meat is tender. Serve with plain boiled rice or plain spaghetti.

(The touch of salad oil, with the butter, prevents butter from becoming too brown and making the kitchen smoky.)

Mrs. Georgina Crane's Maple Syrup Pie

1 cup maple syrup
1 cup milk
2 tablespoons butter

} Heat slowly, stirring constantly, to prevent curdling. Keep below boiling point.

2 egg yolks
1 tablespoon water } beaten together
2 tablespoons cornstarch
⅛ teaspoon salt
1 teaspoon vanilla
dash of pepper (yes, pepper!)

} Mix all this together thoroughly. Add to above and cook until just thickened, not a second longer.

Put this mixture, hot, into a baked pie shell. In making the shell, Mrs. Crane recommends brushing milk over the shell before baking. This makes the crust browner, and also more impervious to the hot filling.

Meringue: Beat the 2 remaining egg whites until stiff, gradually adding 4 tablespoons sugar, ⅛ teaspoon cream of tartar, and dash of salt. The more you beat in the sugar, the less the meringue will "weep." Spread meringue on hot pie filling. Place in preheated 325° oven and bake until meringue is a delicate tan. (Always cool pies on a rack, so that bottom crust does not "sweat.")

This is an old-time, elegant, Vermont favorite, as made by an expert.

POPPY SEED

The only "blue" spice/herb. Yes, the best poppy seed, which comes from Holland, is a sort of slate blue, and though the seeds appear round, they are actually kidney-shaped. Use a magnifying glass and see for yourself. 900,000 seeds = 1 pound. Since ancient times the poppy has been the symbol of fallen warriors; its red flower a reminder of the blood of battle. Strange that poppies grow in Flanders Field, bringing this symbol up to date in the 20th Century. Compared with the ghastly history of opium, the story of the poppy seed is tame. No wars were ever fought over the seeds, but use of them for food and oil goes back to the early ages. The herb probably originated in the Southern European-Western Asian area, but is grown throughout the world today. The fluid in the bud of the poppy, which makes opium, is present only before the seed forms. Seeds are entirely free of a narcotic element. The poppy was cultivated as a source of cooking oil around 1500 B.C. in Egypt. Moslem missionaries took poppy seed to India, where it is a great favorite mixed with sugar to make candy. Used in Jewish holiday cakes. A convenient sort of magic is attributed to the seeds: if put into one's shoes they make one invisible to creditors! Another ancient claim: "The seed easeth the gout...... sleepe, sleepe, sleepe. Stays the flux of the belly and the senses." The "flux of the senses" sounds ominous. Better lay in a large supply of poppy seed.

Poppy Seed in Cooking

Poppy seed has been known for centuries as a flavoring for breads and, as with caraway, makes them more digestible.

Poppy seed, like sesame seed, has its flavor enhanced by baking in a 350° oven for about 15 minutes if it is not going to be baked later. This toasting brings out the nutty flavor and crunchy texture. It's worth the effort.

Use the seeds in cottage and cream cheese, scrambled eggs, over tops of casseroles in place of crumbs, as topping for bread, rolls, cookies. Use in salads. Excellent with fruit.

Make a butter sauce with a generous sprinkling of poppy seeds therein and be sure to heat these together until butter is slightly browned. Pour over fish, green beans, cabbage, potatoes, spinach, carrots, onions, zucchini and all varieties of squash.

The best suggestion of all is to have a generous hand with poppy seed when you serve noodles. Heat the seeds in butter, pour over the cooked noodles, Toss well; a delectable dish is yours.

Carol Ayers' Poppy Seed Salad Dressing

2/3 cup vinegar
1 medium onion, peeled, cut in quarters
2 teaspoons salt
2 teaspoons dry mustard
1½ cups sugar
} Put these ingredients in blender and blend well.

1 cup oil (I use Mazola), added slowly to above, while blending.
3 tablespoons poppy seed

Pour the blended dressing into a glass jar and then, and only then, stir in the poppy seeds! Keep in the refrigerator, well covered. It keeps well and long. If dressing separates, shake well before serving. This dressing makes almost any salad an event, but I like it best drizzled over a tomato-and-white-grape salad. Ditto with avocado and grapefruit.

If you serve this at a party, have the recipe mimeographed. Everyone will ask for it.

Lucille Parker's Poppy Seed Cake

2 cups sugar
1½ cups salad oil (I use Mazola)
4 eggs, beaten
1 teaspoon vanilla
} mixed together in large bowl

3 cups all-purpose flour
1½ teaspoons soda
1 teaspoon salt
} thoroughly mixed together and added alternately to the above, with the evaporated milk, below

1 can evaporated milk (13 ounce)

1 cup pecans, chopped
⅓ cup poppy seeds
} stirred into above batter

Pour into one angel-cake pan or two normal-sized bread pans. (Put greased brown paper in bottom of bread pans.)

Bake at 325° for 50 minutes or longer.

Different, crunchy, delightful.

ROSEMARY

The sea has given rosemary its name: <u>Ros marinus</u> meaning "dew of the sea". It has been called "First Lady of the window garden". One of the world's most wonderful and beloved aromatic herbs. "Restores the mind, averts the evil eye." An evergreen of the mint family, indigenous to the Mediterranean area and said to thrive only in the gardens of the righteous. Rosemary is the symbol of fidelity of lovers, living or dead. Yet Anne of Cleves wore a rosemary wreath on her head when she married Henry the 8th. The symbolism seems not to have held in this case. Not only valued for its symbolism and heavenly scent, but for medicinal and culinary uses. <u>It protects neighboring plants and orchard trees from insects.</u> (Ecologists take note!) Burned in 17th Century courtrooms to protect judges from the pestilences carried by the prisoners who came before them. Until recent years rosemary was burned regularly in French hospital wards to purify and prevent spread of infection. Strewn in clothes closets, it acts as perfume and insect repellent. Has antiseptic qualities. A concoction made from rosemary was called "Queen of Hungary's Water" and was peddled all over the world by gypsies — a cure-all and beautifier. A rosemary bath was called "bath of life." Ancient Greeks believed it fortified the brain and refreshed the memory, so wore rosemary wreaths when taking exams. Appears in every age not only as a brain stimulant but a remedy for heart trouble, to heal wounds, to brighten dull hair and to keep it from falling. No longer considered important as medicine, it is still used widely in cosmetics, soaps, perfumes, deodorants, hair tonics. In Europe herdsmen still pasture animals near rosemary. It imparts a pleasant taste to milk. The herb is dedicated to the Virgin Mary but not named for her as some assume. The herb's love of sea and sun and dew gave it its name as indicated above. Legend has it, however, that on the flight to Egypt Mary threw her cloak over a rosemary bush when the holy family stopped to rest. In the morning the white blossoms had turned blue.

Often planted on graves throughout history: "rosemary for remembrance".

Rosemary in Cooking

Never, never be without this versatile plant in your outdoor garden, in your window garden, on the herb shelf. It has a tenacious, clean, pinetree odor. Despite its versatility it is the most inexpensive of all herbs and spices.

Sprinkle rosemary over the hot coals when barbecuing meat and you will know why Greeks and Romans valued it as incense and why people have always valued it as a meat seasoner.

Throw away expensive household sprays for sweetening the air and burn some rosemary leaves on the kitchen burner or over a candle warmer in any room you wish to make delightfully fragrant.

Make Rosemary Jelly. Make Rosemary Tea and sleep like a baby. Especially good for headache. (See back of booklet.)

Anoint a roasting chicken with salad oil. Sprinkle sparingly with crushed rosemary. Bake to crispness — a uniquely flavored chicken treat.

Always sprinkle rosemary on a leg of lamb when preparing it for roasting, first having squeezed fresh lemon juice over all, then dusted with flour and garlic salt.

Put sprigs of fresh rosemary in the salad bowl.

Add rosemary, fresh or dried, to creamed chicken, soups, stews, and to flavor fish. Add a bit to potatoes while they are boiling. Use rosemary to enhance green beans, asparagus, zucchini, tomatoes. Always use sparingly. One can have too much even of a good thing.

Chicken and Rice, Rosemary (Serves 4)

2 cups diced, cooked chicken
3/4 cup real, uncooked rice
1 cup sliced mushrooms, browned slightly in butter
1/3 cup slivered almonds
1/4 teaspoon dried rosemary, crushed (double if fresh)
1/4 teaspoon dried thyme, crushed ("   "   ")
1/2 teaspoon salt
2 1/2 cups chicken broth

Put all of the above ingredients in a buttered casserole. Stir all together carefully, so as not to break up chicken cubes. Bake, uncovered, in 350° oven for about 50 minutes, or until rice is tender and top a delicate brown. Do *not* stir during baking.

~~~~~~~~~~~~~~

Open Rosemary Sandwiches

Rye bread, sliced very thin and buttered. White meat of chicken or turkey, chopped fine, and mixed with enough mayonnaise to hold the meat together and enough chopped fresh rosemary to season nicely; a bit of salt, to taste. (Dried rosemary may be used, but use less.)

Cut the open sandwiches into any shape desired. Top with slices of stuffed olives. Different, delicate, delicious.

~~~~~~~~~~

Rosemary Lemonade (Serves 6)

1 heaping teaspoon dried rosemary (double this amount if fresh)
1 cup water
1 cup sugar

mixed in a saucepan and boiled gently for 5 minutes. Strain out rosemary and add the liquid to the following ingredients:

3 cups water, 2/3 cup lemon juice, dash of salt. Serve well iced and garnished with thin lemon slices. (Add 1 pint gin or vodka to above if in a party mood.)

~~~~~~~~~~

SAFFRON — The World's Most Expensive Seasoning

It is made of the dried stigmas of the saffron crocus. It takes 75,000 blossoms or 225,000 stigmas for one pound of saffron, so never quibble about the price. It retails in the U.S. at present for nearly $400.00 a pound. Fortunately a little goes a long, long way. It is said to provoke laughter and merriment, is used as medicine, condiment, dye. Its coloring properties have been as prized as its unique flavor. The little crocus is native to the Mediterranean area and is now imported primarily from Spain, where Moslems introduced it in the 8th Century along with rice and sugar. Listed in medical papyrus of Thebes in 1552 B.C. Comes from an Arabic word sounding like "saffron" which means "yellow." King Solomon sang, "A garden inclosed is my spouse... saffron and cinnamon.... frankincense, myrrh.... with all chief spices." Homer spoke of "saffron-robed morning." Saffron was used to scent baths, theaters and public halls of Imperial Rome. Pliny warned that saffron was the most frequently falsified commodity, which is true to this day. Low grade saffron has even been treated with urine to give it color. There are records in the Middle Ages of merchants being burned alive for selling adulterated saffron. Fortunately it is most often falsified with dried calendula or marigold, which is beneficial, and since 1938 we have the Federal Food and Drug Act for protection. But buy the best. A German doctor of the 17th Century claimed saffron could eradicate all sickness from toothache to plague. In India and Far East it is still used as tonic, stomachic, aphrodisiac. In the Dark Ages saffron became lost to England where the Romans had brought it. Then, in the 14th Century, a pilgrim to the Holy Land brought back, at risk of life, one crocus bulb hidden in a hollow staff, from which all English saffron is supposed to descend. At the Time of Richard II saffron was called for in over half of all recipes! Grown in great quantities in Essex and especially in a town called Saffron Walden. The saffron buns of Cornwall are famous. "It maketh the English sprightly", said Francis Bacon.

Saffron in Cooking

Since time immemorial this medicinal and culinary herb has been used in countless dishes: breads, soups, meats, eggs, fish, desserts. In old England the whole meal must have had a yellow cast. Saffron is still used a lot in England today.

Saffron has a great affinity for rice, is always used in bouillabaisse, is particularly good with any chicken dish, and is the secret ingredient of the famous Spanish "Arroz Con Pollo."

Add a pinch of saffron to breads and cakes and cookies — about ½ teaspoon to a recipe of normal size.

Saffron is available powdered or in threads. The latter are usually crushed with mortar and pestle. However, a whole thread or two may be used in the cooking water when boiling rice. Experiment, remembering it is far better to use too little than too much.

Use saffron, and join your fellow man throughout the ages who has doted upon its flavor and color and inducement to good cheer.

Saffron Rice Pilaff

2 ⅔ cups water, brought to a boil in stove-to-table casserole.
¼ teaspoon powdered saffron ⎱ dissolved in above water.
3 chicken bouillon cubes ⎰

⅛ teaspoon garlic powder (not garlic salt) ⎫
sprinkling freshly ground pepper ⎬ stirred into above.
3 tablespoons salad oil ⎭

1 cup best, real, uncooked rice ⎱ stirred into above
⅓ cup seedless raisins ⎰

3 tablespoons shredded almonds, reserved and stirred into the above during last 10 minutes of baking.

Cover and bake in 350° oven for about 45 minutes or until rice is tender. (Don't forget addition of almonds at the last of the baking!)

Serve with chicken, lamb, shrimp, or crabmeat.

Quick Saffron Bread

Slice a loaf of French or Italian bread, diagonally, and in fairly thick slices.

Cream some softened butter with no more than ½ teaspoon powdered saffron.

Spread each slice generously with the saffron butter.

Put the loaf of bread back together again. Wrap in foil.

Heat thoroughly in 400° oven.

Especially good with any fish dish.

SAGE (Salvia officinalis) The Longevity Herb ~ The New England Herb

Like rosemary, it is an evergreen plant of the mint family but has an entirely different flavor. A perennial, to be treasured outdoors and in. Indigenous to Mediterranean area. Sage comes from Latin word meaning "to save" or "to heal" or "to be well." It has always been thought to prolong life and to make one sage and wise. Quotation from Italian medical school at Salerno: "Why should a man die who grows sage in his garden?" The Chinese came to love sage so much when West contacted East in the 17th Century that they would exchange 4 pounds of their best tea for 1 pound of European sage, through the Dutch traders who then held sway. While the Chinese were gratefully sipping sage tea, the British, who had drunk it for centuries, took to avidly drinking the newfound China tea. Another one of those fascinating exchanges. John Wesley claimed that sage tea had proven a remedy for palsy. "My hand is as steady as it was at fifteen," he wrote. It has been venerated as a sacred herb that not only increases life span but has rejuvenating action on eyes, brain, glands. A digestive that cuts the fat in food. The Puritans must have brought it to New England, where it has been thriving ever since. Vermonters still make lots of sage cheese and use it in many pork products. Used in closets for scent and to repel insects; inhalant for congestion of nose and head; a good hair tonic, darkening gray hair and promoting growth; tooth cleanser and gum healer; antiseptic; relieves coughs; a good gargle for sore throats; another one of the cure-all herbs. It is considered the most popular herb in the USA. The very best sage grows wild in Yugoslavia. A superstition concerning sage: "Sage thrives when all is well, droops when misfortune threatens." Sage is a bactericide and fungicide of subtle and penetrating power; and that is no superstition.

Sage in Cooking

This quotation from the "Frugal Housewife" published in 1802 still holds true: "There is no herbe, almost of more use in houses of high and low, rich and poor, for inward and outward occasions... outwardly for bathings.... inwardly for most sorts of broths... to make a sauce for divers sorts of fish and flesh.... to stuff a goose to be roasted." She forgot to mention turkey! Sage is sometimes called "The Turkey Herb." Try to imagine Thanksgiving dinner without sage in the turkey dressing! Sage is the chief ingredient of the famous Bell's Seasoning that has been used in the Thanksgiving bird since time out of mind.

Sage is very aromatic, slightly bitter, and totally wonderful, but is an herb to use with a light hand.

For a tantalizing salad include chopped fresh sage leaves.

Be wise and drink sage tea. You will live longer. Make sage jelly also. (See back of booklet.)

For any food that seems too bland, add a dash of sage. It does wonders.

When my summer herb garden is in full swing I use sage in some way every day. It is a wonderfully satisfying herb. No need to be without it in winter either. It prospers indoors.

Remember: sage offsets fatty foods.

Baked Summer Squash with Sage

A summertime recipe.

Cut a <u>crooked-necked yellow summer squash</u> into thin slices. Arrange slices in a buttered baking dish.

Grate an <u>onion</u> and scatter over the squash.

Chop a handful of <u>fresh sage</u> from the garden and sprinkle over the squash.

Sprinkle with <u>salt and pepper</u>.

Dot with <u>butter</u>.

Bake, uncovered, in preheated 350° oven until squash is tender.

You will never consider summer squash innocuous again.

Watermelon and Sage

This is the most popular, cooling, colorful, crunchy, and light, summertime dessert. Make watermelon balls if you want to be fancy, watermelon cubes if you are in a hurry and feeling practical. Take a handful of sage from the garden and chop it fairly fine. Sprinkle the chopped sage over the watermelon — along with a judicious amount of sugar (or honey). Toss gently, but thoroughly. Pour this into your best glass bowl. Chill.
Your guests' enthusiasm will prove ego-building.

~~~~~~~~~~

Do not discard any left-over sage tea. It gives the greatest boost to a fruit punch.

~~~~~~~~~~

SAVORY

"The bean herb," so called because it goes so well with all sorts of beans. The Germans consider it an essential flavoring for all bean dishes, green or dried, and call the plant "Bohnenkraut" meaning "bean herb". There is _Summer Savory_, the savory of commerce, the one on your herb shelf. It is an annual of the mint family, again from that cornucopia of herb life, the Mediterranean area. There is also _Winter Savory_ which is a hardy, woody perennial. It is less popular than the more delicately flavored Summer variety. Grow it if you want, but remember it is stronger; actually it makes a better house plant than its more delicate sister. Summer Savory (_Satureia hortensis_) was supposed to be the chosen herb of satyrs, probably because it was renowned as an aphrodisiac. Peppery in flavor, it was used a great deal more before pepper reached the Western world. Winter Savory is _Satureia montana_. "Both (Winter and Summer) do marvellously prevail against the winde"... "Will clear the eyes, help deafness and much commended for women with child"... "Stirreth him that useth lechery." Tonic, stomachic, carminative, expectorant, good for bee and wasp stings and for aromatic baths; a bleach for tanned complexions; helps complaints of liver and lungs. Travelled the Rome-to-England-to-the-American-colonies route. Used commercially in perfumes. Grow both varieties outdoors and indoors. If you care to become a buff who dries his own herbs, this is a good variety to start on. A very inexpensive herb, as is rosemary. In Shakespeare's "The Winter's Tale" Perdita says: "Here's flowers for you;
    Hot lavendar, mints, savory, marjoram."

Savory in Cooking

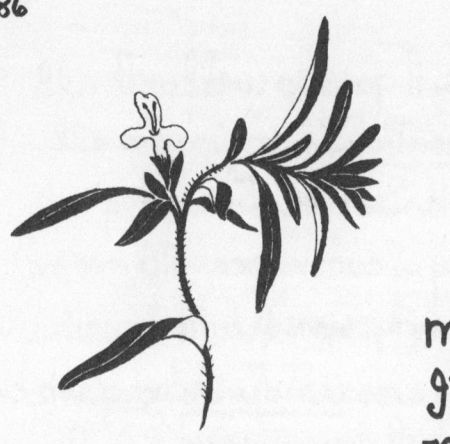

As its name suggests, savory will make a savory dish of almost anything. It was even used in desserts in the Middle Ages, but these days seems more suitable for meat and egg and vegetable dishes, especially beans.

Use a bit of savory with canned beans to take away that tell-tale tinned flavor.

Savory blends well with other herbs. Add it to _bouquet garni_ for soups and stews.

Use the green leaves in salads.

An excellent addition to any fish dish, to scrambled eggs, to hamburgers.

Savory is an important ingredient in poultry seasoning.

Use fresh savory as a garnish and an interesting substitute for parsley.

Savory gives interesting flavor to foods for those on salt-free diets.

Make savory jelly and tea. (See back of booklet for directions.)

Savory Green Beans
(Serves 3 or 4)

1 package frozen green beans (9 ounces)
  cooked by directions on box (or same amount of garden beans)
2 Tablespoons butter, melted, slightly browned
½ teaspoon ground savory (or double amount of fresh)
sprinkle of salt
dash of freshly ground pepper
1 teaspoon lemon juice

Add last four ingredients to melted butter. Pour over hot beans. Toss lightly.

~~~~

Savory Creamed Cabbage (Serves 4 to 6)

1 medium-sized head of cabbage, outer leaves and core removed, and shredded fine. Drop into boiling, salted water, and boil rapidly for 5 minutes only.

2 Tablespoons butter
2 Tablespoons flour } made into a white sauce
1 cup milk

½ Teaspoon crushed, dried savory (Double if savory is fresh.) added to white sauce when it is cooked.

Combine cabbage and sauce in a double boiler. Heat and serve at once. Or allow to cool, uncovered, and reheat at mealtime.

~~~~~

SESAME
— symbol of good luck. "Open Sesame!" Signifies immortality to Brahmins. Negro slaves brought sesame seeds to America and they called them <u>Benne Seeds</u>, by which name they are still known in parts of the South. Early Assyrians, several thousand years B.C., believed their gods drank sesame wine as a prelude to creating the earth. It was food to ancient Egyptians and Persians and a staple as valuable as the soy bean. The seeds are the dried, hulled fruit of a tropical, annual herb indigenous to Indonesia and Africa. Grown for seed, for oil, and also for the leaves, which are eaten in India and Africa. Sesame may be the oldest herb known to man. Sesame seed mash was found recently in Biblical Ararat —— 2,700 years old. The "Open Sesame" of fiction probably derives from the fact that the seeds, when ripe, burst from their pods suddenly, with a sharp "pop" which sounds like a lock springing open. A drawing on an Egyptian tomb of 4,000 years ago shows a baker adding sesame seeds to the dough. Ancient Greek soldiers carried them as energy-boosting emergency rations. Fabulously rich in protein, some of our young people of counter culture, who have given up meat, eat a lot of sesame products for protein reasons. Bread made from sesame and barley flour since earliest times is still made in Iraq today. Total production of sesame seeds is almost 4 <u>billion</u> pounds per year! Most of it is converted into oil, a lovely clear product that rarely becomes rancid, a polyunsaturated fat much used in margarine. The oil is not only fine for cooking but has been used as an all-round medicine and laxative. Recent emphasis on low cholesterol diets has caused a great jump in the demand for sesame. It is imported chiefly from Asia, the Near East, Central America.

Sesame Seeds in Cooking

One of the most versatile seeds — mild, sweet, almondlike in flavor.

Extensively used by Chinese in making candies. Tons of it used in Middle East to make the famous candy — "Halvah."

Seeds may be used in any dish where chopped nuts would be included. What a break — no chopping necessary. Use lavishly.

Seeds come untoasted and may be used without preliminary heating if scattered on top of dishes to be baked. But if seeds are to be incorporated in batters and doughs, or sprinkled on green salads or buttered noodles, they are a thousand times more delicious if toasted first.

To toast sesame seeds: Scatter seeds thinly in a pan. Bake in a 350° oven for about 20 minutes — just until pale tan, no more.

Incorporate 2 tablespoons sesame seeds in one recipe for pastry for the best pie you ever ate. Use 1 to 4 tablespoons, toasted, to 1 pound of hamburger. Use ⅓ cup, toasted, to 3 cups of stuffing for poultry or pork chops. Use 1 tablespoon, toasted, to 2 tablespoons butter for all vegetables. Use 1 tablespoon, toasted, in biscuits and dumplings. Sprinkle over baked goods, having first coated them with beaten egg to make sesame seeds stick. Use in cakes and cookies. Mix with mild cheeses for canapé spread. Use on casseroles in place of crumbs. <u>Use in place of croutons on soup!</u>

You simply can't lose using sesame seeds. One of the greatest boosts to modern (as well as ancient) cuisine and ever so good for you.

Sesame Herb Toast

1 egg, well beaten
¼ pound soft butter
1 tablespoon flour
2 tablespoons sesame seeds
¼ teaspoon dried marjoram } mixed in small bowl
¼ teaspoon dried basil
¼ teaspoon dried rosemary
1 tablespoon dried chives

thin, small pieces of bread
  (I use unbaked Pepperidge Hard Rolls and slice them into thin rounds. Perfect for this recipe.)

Mix all ingredients thoroughly.

Spread on bread until mixture is used up.

Place on cookie sheet and bake in 325° oven until slightly browned.

A very popular canapé.

Equally good served with soup course.

Sesame Wafers (makes about 30 wafers)

½ cup Toasted sesame seeds

1 tablespoon soft butter } creamed together
1 cup brown sugar
3 tablespoons flour
1 egg, beaten
1 teaspoon vanilla extract
½ teaspoon almond extract
¼ teaspoon salt

Mix everything thoroughly, in order given. Drop by small teaspoonfuls onto well-buttered cookie sheets. Bake until firm, five to eight minutes, in preheated 350° oven. Remove from pans while still warm.

~~~~~~

TARRAGON (Artemisia dracunculus)

Teen-ager among the herbs, favorite of French chefs, sometimes called the "Little Dragon", possibly because the word "tarragon" is a corruption of words in other languages meaning "little dragon", perhaps because it is supposed to cure reptile bites, or because the roots of this small perennial of the sunflower family are dragon-like in appearance. Indigenous to Siberia and Western Asia, it has been perfected by the French who seem to appreciate it most. An herb-come-lately to the culinary scene, it is more widely used today than it was in the Middle Ages, which is most unusual. First mentioned by a 13th Century Spanish pharmacist as a seasoning for vegetables, a sleep inducer, a breath sweetener. Not introduced to England until the 16th Century or the U.S. until the 19th. "Tis highly cordial to Head, Heart and Liver," says one old herbalist. All authorities agree that it is best to buy plants, _not seeds_, though the latter are on the market, unfortunately, they say. The French species is best, the Russian less flavorful. So be discriminating and get the best. It's a hardy perennial that should always be in your garden. Dig up some of it for a house plant in winter. It grows gracefully. You will love it. It is used commercially to flavor confectionery, vinegar, pickles, liqueurs, perfumes. Considered a purifier in time of pestilence. One of the strong herbs — to be used with discretion! Great for drying, for pot pourris, dried bouquets. Craig Claiborne cannot praise tarragon highly enough. He says, "Nothing in the repertoire of herbs and spices has a more appealing and seductive flavor than tarragon. It is mysterious, gently pervasive, and is deeply satisfying to the palate." No more need be said.

Tarragon in Cooking

If you have availed yourself of some true French tarragon plants for your garden, you are all set for good eating. Lacking the green plant, buy the best variety of dried tarragon for the herb shelf. This is a festive herb often used by the French on aspic-coated meats.

This versatile and distinguished "gourmets' herb" is used in "fines herbes" and in béarnaise, tartare, and hollandaise sauces.

Use fresh tarragon leaves in the salad bowl, and fresh or dried in soups, stews, sauces.

Tarragon has a special affinity for chicken and lobster dishes.

Good with lamb, in fact with all meats and marinades.

Add a dash to tomato juice and to egg dishes.

In most instances tarragon is best added shortly before cooking time is completed.

Tarragon vinegar is so well known as not to need mentioning.

Tarragon is very aromatic. Be discreet. Better too little than too much.

Baked Tarragon Chicken (Serves 2)

<u>1 cut up frying chicken</u> arranged in buttered, shallow baking dish

<u>Melted butter</u> painted generously over all with a brush
<u>white wine or lemon juice</u> splashed over all
<u>Salt</u> and a little <u>flour</u> sprinkled over all
<u>dried tarragon</u> sparingly distributed over all. Be a bit more generous should you have the fresh variety, chopped.

Bake in 375° preheated oven for one hour, or until beautifully browned. Large pans of this may be prepared for a crowd, but figure one fryer for 2 people.

Try treating a roasting chicken in the same manner, not bothering to stuff or truss it. It needs longer cooking, of course. A refreshing change from traditional roast chicken, and preparation time is only a matter of minutes.

Tarragon Tomatoes (Serves 6 to 8)

<u>5 Tomatoes</u>, cut in half and arranged in shallow baking dish that just holds the halves, nicely snuggled together.

<u>Sugar</u>, just a little, sprinkled over all.

<u>3/4 cup grated cheese</u> (I like old-fashioned "rat-trap" best.)
<u>1/2 cup bread crumbs</u>
<u>1/2 teaspoon salt</u>
<u>1/8 teaspoon freshly ground pepper</u>
<u>1/2 teaspoon dried tarragon</u> (double, if fresh)

} Mixed, and spooned over tomatoes.

Bake, uncovered, in preheated 375° oven for about 1/2 hour.

THYME – *The Manger Herb* –

The Christchild is said to have slept on a bed of hay that contained fragrant thyme. There are said to be some 200 varieties, but <u>Thymus vulgaris</u> is our concern. Thyme is a symbol of activity because bees ever surround it, gathering honey. It is a tiny perennial herb of the mint family, native to Mediterranean area. The name, derived from the Greek, seems to have various meanings: courage, sacrifice, to fumigate. It overruns the pastures of Vermont, a runaway from colonial gardens. Used as incense to perfume and purify ancient temples. The Greeks craved the special honey from Mt. Hymettus where the wild thyme grew thick. "To smell of thyme" was the greatest compliment one Athenian could offer another. Romans bathed in it to acquire courage and strength. In the Middle Ages fair ladies embroidered sprigs of thyme on scarves they gave their knights, to give them courage. Used in "tussie-mussies", small bouquets that ladies carried long ago, holding them so tightly they released a lovely perfume. Used to scent linen. Widely employed in charms and incantations. Among the endless list of ailments it was supposed to cure are: nightmares, melancholy, hangovers, lung trouble, digestive troubles. It is considered a powerful antiseptic and general tonic; and, except for bees, repels insects. Used today in gargles, cough drops, dentifrices, mouthwashes, meat preservatives, anti-mildew preparations. Vets use thyme to cure hookworm in horses and dogs. Said to be under the government of Venus. "Is good against the wamblings and gripings of the bellie, ruptures, convulsions and inflammation of the liver". Thyme is one of the most popular herbs and an important ingredient of "bouquet garni". France is now the leading producer. Thyme helps to give Benedictine its unique flavor. Fortunately the Romans brought thyme to England, as they did literally hundreds of herbs, so that, centuries later, Shakespeare could pen his famous line, "I know a bank where the wild thyme blows."

Thyme in Cooking

Thyme improves many a dish, but there are three things to which it seems especially destined to belong: chicken, New England clam chowder, and onions. Its uses with chicken are legion; just a vague touch in clam chowder does for it what cannot be described but must be tasted. Dare to make creamed onions for 8 people memorable by adding one whole teaspoon of thyme!

As thyme is a part of "bouquet garni", it is a suitable seasoning for all soups and stews, for meats and fish.

Use a touch in clam and tomato and vegetable juice cocktail.

Sprinkle a little in the butter poured over beans, carrots, eggplant, mushrooms, squash, potatoes.

Make thyme tea and jelly. (See back of booklet)

Sprinkle thyme on kitchen burner to make your house smell fresh and beautiful.

Gladys Elviken's Meat-Stretching Rice Jumbo
(Serves 8 to 10)

2 large onions, cut up
2 cups real rice (not instant!)
2 quarts canned tomatoes
½ pound salt pork cut into small pieces, rind removed
1 pound ground beef
2 teaspoons salt
1 teaspoon freshly ground pepper
1 teaspoon Thyme
4 Tablespoons Sugar

Butter a baking dish of proper size to hold all of above ingredients, and mix them well therein. Bake for at least 2 hours at 300°, covered. Stir 2 or 3 times during the baking.

A whole meal in a jiffy, and only one dish soiled! This concoction waits well for company. Can be kept warm indefinitely.

Tuna-Thyme Loaf (Serves 8)

3 (7 ounce) cans tuna fish, drained and flaked
1½ cups soft bread crumbs
⅔ cup of milk
2 eggs, beaten
2 Tablespoons chopped onion
1 teaspoon salt
½ teaspoon garlic salt
2 Tablespoons chopped fresh parsley (or one of dried)
1 teaspoon ground thyme
¼ teaspoon pepper, freshly ground
juice of ½ lemon

Mix all ingredients together thoroughly, in order given. Pack into 1½ quart, buttered loaf pan if you wish to turn it out for serving; —— into a buttered casserole dish if you wish to serve as is. Bake <u>uncovered</u> in preheated 350° oven for one hour, or until browned on top. Serve with egg sauce.

<u>VANILLA</u> is in the orchid class literally and figuratively. It is the third most expensive spice/herb. Vanilla comes from a bean produced by an orchid vine, which grows on a living support of trees or shrubs. The beans are so valuable that, while green and before the harvest, they are "branded" with pinpricks to identify the owner and prevent theft. This is the New World seasoning par excellence, to which the Old World has been indebted since 1520, when one of the officers of Cortez is alleged to have observed Montezuma drinking cocoa flavored with vanilla. Thus vanilla was taken to Europe and cultivated in humid, tropical climates on that side of the world. (Cocoa made its debut, too, of course.) All Europe went crazy over vanilla, especially Queen Elizabeth I. In 1841 Edmond Albius, a former slave on the French Island of Réunion, perfected a quick pollination method, which gave great impetus to vanilla bean husbandry. Even so, the tedious fermentation and curing process of the beans takes about six months. Research continues for speedier methods. There is not enough vanilla to supply world demand, so imitation vanilla flourishes. Never, never, never use it! True vanilla was considered a drug, up to 1910, and also a stimulant, stomachic, aphrodisiac, and antidote to poison. It is now regarded only as the world's most popular flavoring for sweet foods, especially ice cream. Also used in liqueurs and perfumes. Synthetic vanilla is made of wood pulp, waste paper pulp, oil of sassafras, and coal tar. Coumarin, found in the tonka bean and highly toxic, was also used, but is now forbidden by the U.S. Food and Drug Act. Real vanilla is 20 times more costly than the fake product, and worth every cent of it. Today 80% of vanilla comes from Madagascar. Vanilla is not a true spice, so let's call it an herb.

Vanilla in Cooking

Europeans prefer to use the vanilla bean instead of the extract. In the U.S.A. the extract is used almost entirely, though having the bean around is a status symbol among gourmets.

If you want to make the best blueberry pie ever, add the tiniest bit of vanilla to a regular recipe, along with a pinch of cinnamon. Reba Eichlin of Stewartsville, New Jersey, taught me this trick. She made a blueberry pie that was celestial.

Do the same with apple pie, but never so that the vanilla is noticeable. Ditto with blueberry muffins.

Thomas Jefferson stood Washington society on its ear by serving desserts flavored with vanilla. It was an exotic luxury in those days.

Don't bother to cook if you use imitation vanilla. Bakery products and store ice cream are full of it, and they will do just as well for those with defective taste buds.

If a recipe has vanilla as its chief seasoning, double or triple the amount called for. Be as profligate as Montezuma or Thomas Jefferson.

My recipe for plain old boiled custard follows. It is not plain at all, and, kept on hand, it furnishes the makings of many a dessert. The secret of its goodness is a lavish hand with PURE VANILLA EXTRACT.

Old-Fashioned Boiled Custard

4 egg yolks
¾ cup sugar
1½ tablespoons flour
¼ teaspoon salt

} stirred together vigorously in the top of a double boiler.

<u>3 cups milk</u>, scalded, and stirred into above.

Cook over boiling water until custard thickens slightly. Remove from heat at once, or it will curdle. (Stir the custard all the time it is cooking. Don't leave it for an instant!) <u>STRAIN</u> and cool.

1 tablespoon(!) vanilla, stirred into cooled custard. Chill, <u>covered</u> (so it won't form a skin), in refrigerator.

You now have a beautiful, basic, vanilla sauce for countless desserts, in your refrigerator. Please turn the page for suggested uses.

→ → →

Suggested Uses for Boiled Custard

<u>For homemade ice cream</u>: add one quart of cream, 2 more Tablespoons vanilla, about ½ cup more of sugar. Mix and churn. (My father, who made glorious vanilla ice cream every Sunday for 60 years, when taste-testing the creamy custard before churning, always called for "more vanilla, more vanilla!" I believe the total of 3 Tablespoons would match his liberal hand.)

<u>For English Trifle</u>: Line a dish with stale sponge cake, spread cake with raspberry jam, soak it with sherry, top it with Boiled Custard, some whipped cream, and some chopped Macadamia nuts. Prepare at least 12 hours in advance. Refrigerate. Happier guests you will never have.

<u>For Tipsy Pudding</u>: Same as above, except one uses rum instead of Sherry. Any fruit may be used to substitute for raspberry jam.

<u>For Floating Island</u>: Serve custard with a lovely dab of meringue on top.

<u>For Snow Pudding</u>: Custard is a <u>must</u> to go with this light dessert.

The list is endless. Use your imagination. Excellent over all fruits, especially bananas. (Garnish the custard-covered bananas with chopped peanuts.)

Alice Roosevelt Longworth is on record as having disliked boiled custard, in her youth at the White House, because it had "horrid strings of egg in it." Inexcusable! Had the White House chef <u>strained</u> the custard, she would have suffered no such trauma.

Things to Remember about Herbs

Fresh herbs are the best and may be used in greater quantity than the dried variety. Dried herbs are usually about three times as strong as fresh, though some of my recipes have not adhered to this rule. Better to use too little than too much. Herbs are to enhance, not to overwhelm. Use the delicate touch in cooked dishes such as soups, stews, roasts and casseroles. As your experience grows, however, you may lean more on the dictates of your taste buds than on a cookbook.

Usually it is better to add herbs toward the end of cooking. Otherwise they might impart a bitter taste. In seasoning cold foods, use the opposite treatment. The longer they are combined, the more the bouquet grows.

Herbs are a fine substitute for salt for those on a low sodium diet.

There are all sorts of herb mixes on the market. They grow tiresome and have often been on the shelf too long. Be basic and experimental and mix your own. Get to know herbs as an artist knows his pigments.

Keep a well-stocked herb shelf away from too much light and away from heat. Never keep herbs over the stove. Throw out stale herbs and buy a new supply, in small quantities. Time subtracts flavor. Herbs are not expensive, so stop hoarding those dusty bottles!

Herbs are the easiest of all plants to grow and are seldom attacked by pests. Herbs should be cut in the early morning, before the sun dries up their flavorful oils. Gather them for bouquets as well as for culinary purposes. They are not only decorative, but perfume the air.

Ambivalence stalks this subject, for when the herb garden burgeons, one wields a careless hand. Salads are heaped with fresh-chopped herbs, potatoes bathed in parsley, tomatoes blanketed in basil, cucumbers hidden beneath the green lace of dill, fruit cup turned tongue-biting with lavish doses of mint or sage. A good cook, "like the British Constitution,... owes her success in practice to her inconsistencies in principle."

Herb Jelly
(Makes 6 six-ounce glasses. Double recipe if you care to.)

<u>2 cups herb infusion</u>
<u>¼ cup vinegar</u>
<u>4½ cups sugar</u>
<u>food coloring</u>, according to your mood
<u>½ bottle pectin</u> (I use CERTO)

To prepare infusion, pour 2½ cups of boiling water onto 1 cup of well-chopped fresh herbs that have been placed in a non-metal teapot. (You may substitute 4 tablespoons of dried herbs for the 1 cup fresh, if fresh are unobtainable.) Cover teapot and let steep for at least 15 minutes. Strain the infusion and measure 2 cups of same into large kettle. Add vinegar and sugar and cook over high heat, stirring constantly. When sugar dissolves, add coloring. (A light hand with this.) When it comes to a boil, stir in pectin. Bring to a full rolling boil and let it continue, stirring the while, for exactly 1 minute. Remove from heat. Skim off foam. Pour into sterile jelly glasses. Spoon hot paraffin onto jelly at once. Cool, cover, store.

~~~~~~~~~~~~~~~~~~~~

<u>Basil</u>, <u>marjoram</u>, <u>mint</u>, <u>rosemary</u>, <u>sage</u>, <u>savory</u>, <u>tarragon</u>, <u>thyme</u> —— all make fine jellies.

Herb Tea

Herb Teas may be either <u>infusions</u> or <u>decoctions</u> and both should be made in a non-metallic receptacle. The making of an <u>infusion</u> is described on the Herb Jelly page. A <u>decoction</u> is made by combining herb and water, bringing to a boil and allowing to simmer for 15 or 20 minutes.

When using <u>dried leaves</u>, the tea is made by the infusion method. The proportions are about 1 teaspoon to 1 cup boiling water.

When using <u>fresh chopped herbs</u>, the infusion method is used, but use 3 or 4 times more than the dried.

When using <u>seeds</u>, they should be crushed with mortar and pestle. The decoction method should be used, and a heaping teaspoon to 1 cup of water is the average requirement.

You may suit yourself as to the strength of the tea. Tastes differ. Herb Teas are best, sweetened with honey. Never use milk. Lemon is often agreeable.

<u>Herbs Recommended for Tea</u>	<u>The Part Used</u>	<u>Pages to which to Refer</u>
anise	seeds	1 and 2
basil	leaves	5 " 6
caraway	seeds	13 " 14
coriander	seeds	25 " 26
dill	seeds	29 " 30
fennel	seeds	33 " 34
marjoram	whole plant	41 " 42
mint	leaves	45 " 46
parsley	leaves	61 " 62
rosemary	leaves	73 " 74
sage	leaves	81 " 82
savory	leaves	85 " 86
thyme	whole plant	97 " 98

Index of Recipes

Appetizers
- Caraway Spread, 15
- Dill Dip, 31
- Parsley Spread, 63
- Piping Pigs, 51
- Sesame Herb Toast, 91

Beverages
- Cardamom Coffee, 18
- Coriander Coffee, 27
- Herb Teas, 107
- Rosemary Lemonade, 76

Bread
- Norwegian Yule, 20
- Quick Saffron, 80
- Sesame Herb Toast, 91

Cake
- Poppy Seed, 72

Casseroles
- Chicken and Rice, Rosemary, 75
- Meat Stretching Rice Jumbo, 99
- Tuna-Thyme Loaf, 100

Chicken
- Baked Tarragon Chicken, 95
- Chicken and Rice, Rosemary, 75
- Favorite Baked Chicken, 39

Coffee
- Cardamom, 18
- Coriander, 27

Conserve
- Fig Conserve, 3

Cookies
- Anise Wafers, 4
- Coriander, 28
- Fennel Seed, 36
- Sesame Wafers, 92

Desserts
- Cardamom Fruit Cup, 19
- English Trifle, 104
- Floating Island, 104
- Fruit Cup, 18
- Homemade Ice Cream, 104
- Maple Syrup Pie, 68
- Old Fashioned Boiled Custard, 103
- Poppy Seed Cake, 72
- Tipsy Pudding, 104
- Watermelon and Sage, 84

Fish
- Basil Crab Bisque, 7
- Crab Meat Entrée, 43
- Halibut Hollender, 12
- Tuna-Thyme Loaf, 100

Fruit
- Cardamom Fruit Cup, 19
- Fruit Cup, 18
- Lemon-Ginger Fruit, 40
- Pears, Minted, 48
- Watermelon and Sage, 84

Luncheon Dishes
- Basil Crab Bisque, 7
- Chicken and Rice, Rosemary, 75
- Crab Meat Entrée, 43
- Open Rosemary Sandwiches, 76
- Tuna-Thyme Loaf, 100

Ice Cream
- Homemade, 104

Jelly
- Herb Jellies, 106

Meat
- Meat Stretching Rice Jumbo, 99
- Veal Scallopine, 67

Mustard
- Hot Mustard, 51
- Mustard Sauce, 52

Index of Recipes

Pie
Maple Syrup, 68

Potatoes
Cardamom Sweet Potatoes, 19
Fennel Potatoes, 35
Irish Champ, 55
Potato Salad with Cucumber and Basil, 8

Relish
Garden Relish, Pickled, 60
Lemon Carrot Relish, 40
Lemon-ginger Fruit, 40
Minted Pears, 48

Rice
Chicken and Rice, Rosemary, 75
Meat Stretching Rice Jumbo, 99
Saffron Rice Pilaff, 79

Salad Dressing
Poppy Seed, 71
Texas Celery Seed, 23

Salad
Dill-icious Cabbage, 32
Marinated Green Beans, 44
Pickled Garden Relish, 60
Potato, 8

Sandwiches
Open Rosemary, 76

Sauces
Hot Mustard, 51
Mustard Sauce, 52

Soup
Basil Crab Bisque, 7
Broccoli, 59
Greek, 39
Parsley, 64
Senate Bean, 11

Tea
Herb, 107

Vegetables
Artichokes, Boiled, 27
Beans, Green with Marjoram, 44
Beans, Savory Green, 87
Beets, Caraway, 16
Cabbage, Savory Creamed, 88
Celery, Braised Hearts, 24
Celery, Double Boiler, 23
Irish Champ, 55
Onions, Basic Baked, 56
Peas, Minted, 47
Potatoes, Fennel, 35
Potato Salad with Cucumber, 8
Rice Pilaff, Saffron, 79
Spinach, Quickee, 44
Squash, Baked Summer, 83
Sweet Potatoes, Cardamom, 19
Tomatoes, Tarragon, 96